BRAZILIAN JIU-JITSU
ULTIMATE FIGHTING TECHNIQUES

Volume 1: The Top Game

Royce Gracie

with
Kid Peligro

INVISIBLE CITIES PRESS • MONTPELIER, VERMONT

Invisible Cities Press
41 Northfield Street
Montpelier, VT 05602
www.invisiblecitiespress.com

Library of Congress Cataloging-in-Publication Data

Gracie, Royce.
Ultimate fighting techniques / Royce Gracie with Kid Peligro.
p. cm. -- (Brazilian jiu-jitsu)
ISBN 1-931229-36-8
1. Jiu-jitsu--Brazil. I. Peligro, Kid. II. Title. III. Series.
GV1114.G78 2005
796.815'2--dc22
2005001688

Anyone practicing the techniques in this book does so at his or her own risk. The
authors and the publisher assume no responsibility for the use or misuse of information contained in this book or for any injuries that may occur as a result of
practicing the techniques contained herein. The illustrations and text are for
informational purposes only. It is imperative to practice these holds and techniques under the strict supervision of a qualified instructor. Additionally, one
should consult a physician before embarking on any demanding physical activity.

Printed in the United States of America
Book design by Peter Holm, Sterling Hill Productions

CONTENTS

INTRODUCTION

For years my fans have asked me for a book that would teach them the full spectrum of moves that have allowed me to be so effective in the world of No-Holds-Barred fighting. This is that book. To do that subject justice and present a truly thorough explanation of my game, I have divided the information into two volumes. This book focuses on the top game. Volume 2 will focus on the bottom game.

It may surprise you how much I concentrate in these pages on the fine details of the foundational jiu-jitsu positions. Getting those basic moves exactly right has been the secret of my success. There's a reason those moves are basic—it's because they're so effective! I rarely bother with exotic moves in a fight. I know that the difference between victory and defeat is in doing the moves right—and doing them right means paying great attention to issues of timing, placement, and quick decision making. Those are the skills I'll teach you in this book.

The techniques presented in this book are the simple, high-percentage moves that work! They work whether you are in the academy sparring, on the streets in a self-defense situation, or in the midst of a No-Holds-Barred match. Many of them are neglected by some students and instructors, as they seek to learn more complex moves that in their eyes hold the key to success. While complex moves are important to know, the situations where they can be used seldom occur. Too often we complicate our jiu-jitsu with too many movements and techniques. The "basics" is all we really need. It is our lack of solid basics that many times puts us in trouble and forces us to have to try a low-percentage, complex move. Fancy or new moves are by no means bad; I think innovation is good for the sport, and every now and then a new position comes along that really does change the game. But if we really think through our jiu-jitsu and have a very good understanding of the principles, we will have the advantage in 99 out of 100 situations. Mastering the techniques presented in this book will allow you to form a foundation that will be carried all the way past your black belt.

Gracie Jiu-Jitsu Philosophy

Gracie jiu-jitsu is a martial art that works on the principle of action and reaction. That is the beauty of the art; rather than fight against force, a Gracie jiu-jitsu practitioner learns to use the opponent's power against him. You know that if you push someone they will push back, so if you want them to come to you, rather than pulling them to you (to which they'll react by pulling away), why not push them slightly? When they react against the push, then you have them where you want them. That is action and reaction. If you want to pry an opponent's arm away from his body, try pushing the arm against his body. The reaction will be to try to extend the arm, and that is exactly what you wanted in the first place. Gracie jiu-jitsu is based on this simple idea, action-reaction, leverage and base.

Imagine a head on attack on a powerful fortress—a big mistake in most cases. Now imagine sending a small group to the front to get attention, while sneaking an assault force around the blind side! That is what jiu-jitsu is about: cunning, intelligence, and surprise. Jiu-jitsu is a chess game with your body, where you use every element available to defeat your opponent. You need to use your arms, legs, fingers, feet and toes, vision, mind, intelligence, sense of touch, vision, and hearing—everything you have—because you are not fighting against a machine but rather against the greatest fighting device ever created—another human being!

Using this action-and-reaction principle is more important than knowing a thousand techniques without a reason. While beginners see learning many techniques as progress, the reality of Gracie jiu-jitsu is that you do not need to have a vast array of techniques in your arsenal. What you need to have is a solid foundation of techniques that you know very well and are able to use properly. It is more important to understand how and when to use a certain technique than to know several different attacks for the same position. That is why it takes quite a bit of time on the mat for a person to advance in Gracie jiu-jitsu.

Jiu-jitsu is not like a cake recipe with well-defined, step-by-step instructions. Instead, it involves thousands of different possibilities to each sequence of moves. As you learn more and more moves, little by little, if you are training with a reasonable amount of awareness and good instruction, you and your body will naturally select what works for you and what should be your game. Different body types should have different arsenals. A tall person with long legs, for instance, will play the closed guard very well and have a good triangle, while a person with short legs may have a much better open guard and guard replacement, and his triangle may not be as effective. A strong and bulky person may be able to control from the top better, but will most likely leave more spaces for escapes than a smaller person.

When learning jiu-jitsu, at every stage—especially the initial ones—the goal is to learn many moves, but not be obsessed with the idea that progress is measured by the number of moves that you know. Many great fighters are very successful with a small array of moves, because they do them so well and are able to select the proper weapons for each situa-

Royce keeps Yoshida at a safe distance with a kick.
Pride Shockwave, December 31, 2003. Susumu Nagao photo.

tion. In jiu-jitsu it is much better to be a master of few trades rather than a jack of all! If you look at my performances in various NHB matches, I used very few "advanced" or "sophisticated" moves. I used the basic moves of Gracie jiu-jitsu (most of which are shown in this book) to defeat opponents that were bigger and more powerful than me.

Today, too many fighters are obsessed with fancy moves and never learn the basics. At a tournament recently, a white belt was using a very sophisticated guard and giving his opponent a hard time. But it turned out that was the only move he knew. Once the guy on top passed his guard, he quickly mounted and submitted the white belt. Many of today's fighters have skipped over the basics and proceeded to advanced moves. That isn't a problem if they fight mirror images of themselves, but when they face more complete fighters, their weaknesses are glaring. How else can you explain the fact that many advanced competitors fall for the most basic chokes and armlocks?

Don't worry about learning many new moves. Instead, practice and understand the moves you do know to the point that they are "in your blood," as I like to say. How do you achieve that point of having the techniques be in your blood? There are six steps:

1. Static repetition with a willing partner.
2. Limited-scope drills in which only certain movements are allowed.

3. Open sparring against less technical or weaker opponents.
4. Open sparring against equal opponents.
5. Open sparring against better opponents.
6. Competition.

Let's analyze each of these steps.

1. Static repetition against a willing partner. This means repeating a move over and over against a willing partner—say, an elbow escape ten times to each side, three times a week. On the first repetitions, your partner should cooperate fully with you, then gradually increase the degree of difficulty as you progress with the move. If you have just learned a move, there is no way for you to repeat it correctly in a stressful situation, so the best way to learn the basic mechanics of the move is to repeat it against a willing partner. The positive thing about this stage is that you learn to execute the move. The drawback is that even when your partner tries to increase the degree of difficulty, he cannot really simulate an actual sparring session. Also, when things are really moving, different difficulties appear.

2. Limited-scope drills in which only certain movements are allowed. This means drilling a position over and over. When a predetermined result occurs, you start over. An example here is passing the guard when the opponent cannot use his hands to defend the pass. Once you pass, or if you get caught in a submission, you start over. The advantage here is that you can drill a situation over and over, including situations that may not happen frequently in a match or sparring session, such as attacking from the mount. When two people of equal skills train together, they won't often get the opportunity to mount one another. How are you going to develop your ability to maintain the mount or attack from the mount if the moment you mount your opponent he escapes? This drill will assure that you repeat the situation many times, allowing you to learn its intricacies and nuances. Depending on the limitations imposed, you will develop or emphasize certain aspects of the game. In the guard pass, for example, the passer develops his passing skills, while the defender learns to use his legs to defend. Since the defender has limited use of his body, his task is more difficult and he may end up failing and having his guard passed, but as you allow him to use one or both hands, he will find that he can defend the guard better and has really learned how to use his legs. The shortcoming of this drill, again, is that due to the limited scope of the training you may not develop the ability to reach the positions in a dynamic environment. Once everything is open, situations are never exactly the same; that type of environment can only be achieved with regular sparring.

3. Open sparring against less technical or weaker opponents. This is a perfect situation for you to practice new moves. The upside of sparring against lesser opponents is that you can control the training, to a certain extent. Since you have the upper hand in technical skills, you can direct the training to specific areas that you want to improve. For example, when you learn a new move, you may never get the opportunity to use it against a better opponent. Even if the opportunity arises, your mastery of the move may not be good enough to pull it off. Your opponent will defend it, and as a result you may end up in a precarious position. After a few unsuccessful tries, you give up on the move entirely, because in your mind, it just doesn't work. Now, if you are training against a lesser partner, the move may fail the first time, but since you control the training with your better skills, you can get back to the same situation and repeat the move until it becomes successful. Since your opponent is not as adept, his reaction to the move will be less precise, giving you a better chance of success. If your partner is not as strong as you, you can also muscle in and out of situations. Although that is not the object of Gracie jiu-jitsu, at times strength is helpful until you learn the proper dynamic mechanics that make a move work.

This is also a good time to improve your defensive skills. By letting yourself get in precarious positions, like being mounted or having someone on your back, you will be able to learn how to escape these situations against opponents who do not present a great threat, allowing you to not only learn the nuances of the escapes but also to relax and think clearly while under duress.

The downside of this training is that you may get a false sense of security. You may become accustomed to success and shy away from failure, and begin to avoid training against better partners for fear of being submitted or challenged by them. The ego is a great hinderer of progress. Don't let it hinder you. Always remain humble.

4 and 5. Open sparring against equal and better opponents. After mastering a move against lesser opponents, the next step in furthering your knowledge is to try these moves against equal opponents, and then against better ones. This will reveal weaknesses and strengths in your techniques, so that you can go back to step 3 and finesse them even more, or get help from your instructor. The progress here may be slower than in the prior steps, but it is necessary that you work these techniques against opponents of increasing skill and strength so that you master the

Royce executes a side-kick before coming in on Art Jimmerson. UFC I, November 12, 1993. Royce Gracie personal archives.

technique and can use it against anyone you face. The key here is to be realistic with your expectations and not get discouraged because your success ratio is less than before. With practice, you will soon be pulling off these moves against even the best and strongest opponents.

6. Competition. Competition is the ultimate testing ground for any athlete. While it isn't essential that you compete, preparing for a competition will turbo charge your progress in the art. The narrow focus of preparing for a match—winning by either points or submission—will sharpen your moves and exacerbate your weaknesses so that you will easily see what needs to be worked on. Many times, the preparation for the competition itself is the most important part of this step. However, by competing against another fighter, you will be able to see how you react to an extreme situation. Being in a match is the closest thing there is to being in a real fight! This will develop your ability to control your emotions and learn to deal with your fears and anxiety, leaving you much more relaxed and confident for any real-life confrontation.

Training

While some people correctly point out that in a street fight, no one asks you if you are ready, in order to get the most out of training you need to ready your mind and body to the task ahead. It is very important to do stretches and warm-up exercises prior to training in order to lubricate your joints, muscles, and mind.

If you develop a pre-training routine that is effective and consistent, you will always be ready to do your best. Warm-ups should include doing circular motions with most of the body joints, such as hips, knees, ankles, shoulders, elbows and wrists. Stretches should involve all or most of the major muscles that are going to be used in the training. A great reference to these stretches and warm-up exercises can be found in my book *Superfit*.

After the warm-ups, a series of drills should be performed, such as hip escapes, upas, armlocks from the guard, and "toreana" guard passes. This is a great way to get your mind into the task ahead. Once you complete the warm-ups and drills, you should be ready to spar and be your best.

Remember that your training partners are key to your success and improvement in the art. Unlike other martial arts where one can perform katas and practice sequential moves in isolation, jiu-jitsu involves action and reaction that can only be fully implemented when used against an opponent. You cannot learn to do a sweep without interacting with an opponent's body and his reaction to the move. You cannot learn to do a hip throw without learning where hips have to fit in relation to your opponent's hips to have the proper control and leverage for the move to work. Consequently, it is extremely important for you to have a good relationship with your training partners, to view training as an intrinsic and fun part of learning, and to understand the etiquette of sparring.

Many practitioners view sparring as a must-win situation and put an unnecessary amount of effort into winning every session. While there are occasions when you want to train hard with the objective of winning, many of your best training sessions, where you learn the most, are the ones where your effort and concentration are directed toward learning without regard for score or final success. By viewing every sparring session as a must-win situation, you may alienate partners that could add a lot to your growth. Additionally, if you train hard every time, you will greatly increase your chances of injuring yourself or your partner. If you develop a reputation as someone who is out of control, you may end up with an ever-shrinking pool of willing partners, making it impossible to get the variety of training that is necessary to develop all parts of your game.

So you should view your training sessions as learning experiences, leaving the pressure of results to the competition or the street. Your training should be directed toward perfecting the moves that you've learned, sharpening your timing, and increasing your understanding of the game in its totality. Conduct yourself in training with respect for your opponent and respect for yourself. Live by the Golden Rule. Don't do anything to your opponent that you wouldn't want done to you!

Objectives of Training

Set a goal at every training session to improve some part of your game. Having a set of loose objectives or guidelines for training will greatly help your progress and shorten your learning curve. If you view every sparring session the same way, you may not take advantage of several things that are important to learn. Rather than just go into a sparring session without a purpose, try having an objective training session each time. Objective training means that in most training sessions you have one or several objectives in your agenda, much like in life you have objectives for each day, each week, and each year. While there are too many objectives to be listed, and most of the time these options are flexible and dependent on your individual characteristics, certain objectives are common to most practitioners. These are presented below as a guide for you to understand, modify, adapt, improve, and improvise your own particular list of objectives.

1. Pay attention to your opponent's weight. By watching where your opponent distributes his weight, you will be more aware of what moves will and will not work, especially sweeps and reversals. If your opponent has his weight back, for instance, it may be better to come up on him with a cross-over sweep than an overhead sweep. If your opponent is leaning to the right, it will be easier to go that way than to try and use a move that forces him to the left, as you will have to force his weight clear across. It is much more effective to use your opponent's weight to assist your move than to go against the weight.

2. Pay attention to your opponent's preferences. Many people have a dominant side. They prefer to do things to that side, like passing to the left or attacking across-side from the right. Many have a sweep they prefer, or like to attack the arm or the neck. Pay attention to what your opponent's preferences are. This will help you learn your opponent's game quickly and adjust to it so you can avoid his strengths and take advantage of his weaknesses. After you learn your opponent's preferences, try crossing him up. If he prefers to pass to the left, try forcing him to pass to your right. This is extremely important in a competition or street fight, where you don't have the luxury of spending time trying to figure out what works. In a street fight, efficiency is the key to success. The faster you can solve your aggressor's puzzle, the better your chances of success. Conversely, in sparring, occasionally try going at your partner's strengths. This will force you to perfect your moves against the best that he has to offer.

3. Train with an open mind. Many people, especially novices, go into a training session with a certain move that they expect to use. Many times it is a move they have just learned or something that they feel comfortable with, like pulling guard at the opening of the sparring session. The problem here is that your partner has his own ideas, which may not match yours. As soon as the session starts, you get crossed up and cannot recover from your broken plans! There is nothing worse than coming into a sparring session or a match thinking, "I am going to start off pulling guard and attack his arm with that cool armlock I just learned," only to have your opponent pull guard on you first!

It is a sign of training maturity to go into a training session without any preset moves or strategies. That does not mean that you cannot have a general strategy against a specific partner or competitor, but if you enter with a firmly set plan, you may be in trouble. Stick to loose objectives such as "today I want to work on my defense" or "today I want to work on my sweeps," but flow with the situation, much like water flows around a rock placed in its path. If you move the rock, the water doesn't fight it or think, "Darn, my path is blocked. I was hoping the rock would be on the other side." The water just flows around the situation!

4. Train with novices. Although many people think that training with novices is a waste of time and a recipe for injuries due to their lack of control, training with novices serves important tasks in your evolution into becoming a jiu-jitsu expert. When you constantly train with people who are practitioners of the art, their reactions to moves are within the scope of techniques that are taught and practiced every day. They make sense, and therefore are somewhat predictable. An untrained opponent, on the other hand, may do anything. Many of his moves may not be terribly effective, but the element of surprise can certainly throw you off guard. A street fight is an unpredictable thing and you should expect the unexpected. By training with a newer fighter, you will develop your reactions to unexpected moves and be better prepared for an altercation.

Another reason to train against beginners is that, since most people train regularly in a certain academy, you tend to advance with your peers. After a while, the technical evolution almost appears to stop. The same people still give you the same hard times, and you start to wonder if you are progressing at all. When you train with a newer student or even a friend who has not practiced jiu-jitsu, you will suddenly see your evolution. You will also realize that the techniques you've learned work! It can be very gratifying.

5. Train with a variety of partners. Training with different partners will develop your game in a more complete way. Some partners have different strength and weaknesses, different body types and speed, thereby forcing you to develop many different facets of your game. If you constantly train with the same people you will, after a short while, almost synchronize your moves to their moves. You will begin to limit your game to the things that work best against those people. For instance, if they defend the guard well, when you pass low, you will use standing guard passes and avoid the other ones. If they escape the mount well, you will only attack from across-side. In contrast, training with different people will force you to develop the entire gamut of techniques. Having a variety of training partners will develop your ability to adjust your game to different opponents and situations, making you a much more complete fighter.

On the other hand, there are some benefits to training with the same partners regularly as well. When you train all the time together, your partner's reactions to your moves are slightly faster than anyone else's, because he knows your game. That forces you to be sharper and faster to stay ahead of him. You will find that often the people you train with the most are your toughest opponents. When you train with others, sometimes of even higher technical skills, you'll often have a much higher rate of success, because they don't have that familiarity with your game. Another big advantage of training with regular partners is that you will not get injured as much.

6. Relax. One overlooked factor in achieving technical advancement is the ability to relax while training. How can anyone sense the reaction of an opponent if he is too tense himself? Progress can be measured as one's ability to relax in training and in performance situations. If you are tense, you use up a lot of energy and you are not able to think clearly. If you are not able to think clearly, you are not going to be able to anticipate your adversary's attacks or to formulate a solution for the situation you are in.

This applies even more when you are on defense. The typical example is being mounted. If you are tense, all you can think about is getting out

Royces shoots low on Ken Shamrock. UFC I, November 12, 1993. Royce Gracie personal archives.

of the position as quickly as possible. So you explode and do an upa (bridge), maybe extend your arm, and get caught in an armlock, or expose your neck to the choke because in your haste to escape you didn't feel the opponent's hand deep in your collar. A situation like this calls for relaxation and clear thinking. Often you'll find yourself in a tough place, but have managed to defend and stabilize the position, such as a double attack that you have neutralized. Once you have assured yourself that the danger is over, you should remain calm and let the attacker make the next move. If you make an attempt to escape, you may give the attacker the opportunity to come back and finish you, while if you remain patient and focus on defense, your opponent will eventually change his attack, allowing you a greater opportunity to escape. Once you have protected yourself from the choke or armlock or punch, and you know your opponent cannot hurt you, then you are able to relax and survey the situation at hand. Where is my opponent's weight? Does he have his knees tight against my body? Are his hands busy gripping something? If so, maybe the proper escape is the upa. Since his knees are tight and his hands are busy, a bridge would resolve the situation. How are you going to be able to do this type of reasoning if you are tight and exasperated?

Recently I watched a local NHB fight show. The show was great and

Attacking the turtle. Royce talks to the referee while controlling Ken Shamrock. UFC I, November 12, 1993. Royce Gracie personal archives.

the local fighters were enthusiastic and skilled. The thing that struck me the most, however, was that, despite the fact that they were fighting 3 x 3 minute rounds, most of them were completely gassed before the end of the fight.

Think about it. Nine minutes is not even the first round in a Pride match. They were getting tired before the end of the first round! Of course a lot of that can be attributed to inexperience and excitement, but, from what I could see, a lot was due to the fact that they fought so hard and so tense the entire time. Sure, it's hard to fight relaxed when the opponent is trying to take your head off, but the problem with most fighters is that they make things harder on themselves. They fight hard and then are spent at the end of a three-minute round. Whether you are fighting an NHB match, a BJJ tournament, or just sparring with your friends at the school, it is important for you to be able to relax.

How do you relax? Having good technical positions will certainly help. If you have proper techniques and good posture, you should be able to use less power and more leverage, which will help you relax. Begin training without grabbing the gi so hard. Place your hands and arms in positions where the angle and leverage are best. If you know the right way to defend an attack, you will use a lot less energy, both physical and mental, than if you just struggle and power your way out.

If you are in a street fight or a no-time-limit match and you run out of gas, you are in trouble. You should strive to fight every fight as if there is no time limit. If you get in that frame of mind, then you will have to relax, and by relaxing not only will you fight longer, but you will also feel the situation a lot more.

Injuries

Injuries are a part of every sport and martial arts is no different. Striking martial arts lead to a lot of injuries, such as broken noses, feet, and hands. In jiu-jitsu, because of the lack of strikes, one can train in very realistic ways while minimizing such injuries. That is not to say, however, that injuries are rare in jiu-jitsu. Sprained elbows from armlocks and sprained fingers from getting caught in the gi are fairly common grappling injuries. If you are constantly getting injured, you are weakening yourself. The injuries often don't heal as well as before. In addition, if you are constantly getting injured, you will start wanting to avoid practicing. You will lose one of the best aspects of jiu-jitsu, which is having fun while training.

Minimizing injuries can be done if you train intelligently. First, do not resist submissions to the point of injuring yourself. While this may sound reasonable, many times, because of human nature and pride, students will resist the submission attempt and end up with an injured limb. Be smart when training. Know your limits and remember that the important thing is not to win every training session, but to learn the techniques and be able to train regularly. The academy is not the street and a sparring session is not a life-or-death situation, so learn to submit and start over.

Avoid training with reckless partners. In your career you will undoubtedly encounter people who always train recklessly, because of their nature or simply because of lack of knowledge. Such people should be avoided at all costs. Stay away from them and you will reduce your injuries tremendously.

Sometimes the problem of injuries lies with us. If you find that other students avoid training with you, or you are always involved in injuries either to yourself or your partner, it may be time to take a look at yourself and see if you are the problem. Are you out of control when going for submissions? Are you too tense when training? Try analyzing the situation, asking your academy friends for advice, and especially talk to your instructor and find out what the problem is and ways to correct it.

Another very important aspect of avoiding injuries is to protect yourself at all times. Much like an NHB referee will instruct the fighters, "Gentlemen, protect yourself at all times!" this is a must when sparring and competing. If you find yourself in an awkward position, try adjusting your body so that no injury can occur. If your arm gets caught in a weird position, adjust it so that it is protected, even if you have to give up position. While that may sound contrary to the philosophy of maintaining or bettering position at all times, think about it for a minute: you are in a street fight, your arm gets caught in an awkward place, but yet you don't want to give an inch to your aggressor, so you hold the position and resist the move and BAM! Your arm is broken or dislocated. Instead of giving up a position and recovering later, now you have to fight with a broken arm!

Positional Hierarchy

Because of jiu-jitsu's incredible flexibility, you can strike quickly from an almost limitless variety of positions. Still, there is a general consensus that some positions have more advantages than others. Here is a list of positions, from worst to best:

- Opponent is on your back
- Opponent is mounted on you
- Opponent has side-control
- Opponent is on top in your half-guard
- Opponent is in your guard
- You are in his guard
- You are on top in his half-guard
- You have side-control
- You are mounted on your opponent
- You have taken his back

While this may seem like a sequence to be followed, jiu-jitsu is a dynamic sport with many shortcuts that can quickly change the situation and danger of submission. For instance, you may have taken someone's back, but with proper escape techniques he can end up on side-control on you. So, while achieving a certain position is important, it is more important to maintain the position and even more important to have proper posture at all times. For example, say your opponent has taken your back, but he overextends his arm and is submitted. He went from best position to worst in one instance, because he failed to maintain proper posture and keep his arms close to his body at all times.

Fundamentals

To become a great jiu-jitsu practitioner, you have to master the fundamentals. While you can have knowledge of a large variety of moves and even be able to execute many of them in dynamic situations, you will not be able to survive against top-level fighters if you don't have the proper fundamentals down. Much like a child first learns to crawl before he can walk, and then walks before he can run, a jiu-jitsu practitioner needs to master the basics before he can venture out into exotic or specialized moves.

If you observe two athletes sparring, you will see that they spend a majority of their time either passing or defending the guard. Thus, a good jiu-jitsu game begins with a strong foundation in those skills.

To pass the guard, one has to have proper base and posture. Base can be defined as the ability to maintain balance and be centered. Staying in base while standing or in someone's guard generally means having your weight spread equally between the support points.

Proper posture is another key to success in Gracie jiu-jitsu. One cannot achieve dominance of a position, nor the ability to relax when in a difficult position, without having proper posture. In general, proper posture means having your limbs close to your body, having your elbows close to your chest, and maintaining a straight line between your spine and your head. First, let's look at a few top-game situations and examine the elements of proper posture.

An omoplata will tame the biggest opponent—even someone more than twice your weight! Royce versus Akebono, K-1 Dynamite, December 31, 2004. Photo courtesy K-1.

Side-control bottom

Pedro's legs are bent and ready to bump or initiate an escape.

Pedro's right arm is bent with the elbow and the forearm bracing against Royce's hips to keep distance.

Pedro's left arm is under Royce's right armpit.

Side-control top

Royce's chest is 90° with Pedro's chest and pressing against it.

Royce's right hand is on the mat next to Pedro's right hip to prevent him from replacing the guard.

The low leg has the knee curled and next to Pedro's hip to prevent him from replacing the guard.

Royce's left arm is bent at the elbow with the elbow pressing tight against Pedro's left ear to deny him any space to turn his head. If Pedro can't turn his head, he cannot turn his body to the side either.

Royce's high leg is stretched out.

Royce's left toes are pressing against the mat, ready to spring him to action.

Posture in the guard

Royce's head is perfectly perpendicular to the ground. If Gui tries to pull the collar to break his balance, Royce counters by leaning back with his head.

Royce's eyes are looking straight. Should Royce look down, he woud lose posture.

Royce's back posture has his spine in a straight line.

Royce's left hand (not shown) grabs Gui's belt, with the elbow tight and over Gui's hip.

Royce sits on his heels.

Royce's knees are close, but not too tight against Gui's hips. They are just wide enough to give him balance without being wide open.

Royce's right hand grabs both Gui's collars and presses down slightly on the chest. Should Gui attempt to sit up, Royce will put pressure on the arm, preventing him from getting up.

Opponent mounted

Royce's knees are up as high as possible with the feet firmly planted on the mat, ready to bump or bridge.

Royce's hands are in a defensive position, ready to block any punches to the face or catch Pedro's hands trying to grab the gi collar.

Royce's elbows are low, preventing Pedro from riding up on him with his knees

Mounted on opponent

Torso should be erect unless going for an attack. Notice the shoulder is square and Royce is neutral, not leaning forward or back.

Royce's head is straight and his arms are at his sides.

Don't sit on your opponent. Keep your hips slightly off his body.

Royce's knees should be close to his torso, not wide. Also, his knees should be as high up towards the armpit as possible.

Opponent on your back

Royce has his right arm wrapped around his head, blocking Pedro from attacking the collar with his right hand. That is the side Royce will escape to.

Pedro's left hand on the collar doesn't concern Royce, as he is escaping towards his right.

Royce uses his left hand to grab Pedro's right wrist to further limit his ability to attack the right side.

Notice Pedro's incorrect posture with the feet crossed.

On opponent's back

Royce's chest is close, pressing against Gui's back, and his head is on the side opposite to the attacking arm (in this case, the left arm).

Royce's feet are not crossed and the hooks are not too deep (i.e., he is pressing the lower half of his calf against Gui's thighs). If Royce has his legs up to his knees, he is too deep.

Royce's hips are square behind Gui without leaning to one side or the other, giving him equal attack opportunities to either side.

Hips Close to the Joints

A few words more should be said about hip position. Generally, in order to get a submission lock, your hips should be close to the joint that you are attacking. For example, if you want to do an armlock from the guard, one of your first concerns should be to have your hips high up on the opponent's armpits, thus near his elbow joint. If you attempt to do the same armlock with your hips far from the joint, he will easily escape, or you won't be able to apply pressure to the joint in question. For chokes, you generally want to have the opponent's neck and head close to you. Again, if you want to catch him with a collar choke from the guard, you should pull his head to your chest, rather than try choking him from afar.

Maintaining Position

One of the most misunderstood things in jiu-jitsu is positional control. Maintaining position is one of the keys to success in sparring, street fights, and NHB matches. Many times a person, in his haste to either advance or submit his opponent, will lose control of the position and yield ground to the opponent. Maintaining position does not mean statically holding your opponent in place using your strength, but rather being able to adjust and flow while applying your weight to keep your opponent under control.

Many examples can be cited to illustrate this. For instance, say you are passing someone's guard using the toreana pass and have almost reached side-control. You let go of the legs and quickly try to drive your chest onto your opponent's chest to achieve side-control, however, as you let go of the legs, he either turns to all fours or quickly replaces the guard. Another example: You have mounted your opponent and try quickly to choke him without properly adjusting your weight and hips. He bridges and rolls you over, ending up in your guard. In both situations, all the effort used to achieve a good position was wasted because you failed to maintain control of the position. There is nothing more frustrating and exhausting than to lose a dominant position after all the effort it took to get there. In Brazil we like to say, "You swam and swam but drowned on the beach!"

It is much more important to retain your gains than to risk them all in a big leap and end up with a setback. In Gracie jiu-jitsu, minute gains and adjustments are often keys to final success. If you are steadily advancing and maintaining positional control, as your opponent's position becomes more precarious he will get more and more uncomfortable and desperate, and many times will make a bold move to escape the pressure, giving you a great opportunity to submit him or gain an even better position. Your opponent should feel like he is holding a large boulder from rolling down a hill. The weight is on him at all times; he can sustain the pressure for a while but inevitably he will succumb. At first he struggles and makes small adjustments. His legs are getting tired, so he takes a step back. As he takes the step back, the boulder just keeps rolling slowly down the hill, and the pressure remains the same or worse. At some point he will either try to jump out of the way or get run over by the boulder.

You, the boulder, need to be ready for his jump, to know where he is going to jump and take advantage of the opening, but the whole idea is to maintain control of the situation and apply pressure all the time.

How do you apply pressure? It depends. Generally, if you are passing or across-side, your chest should be pressuring your opponent and you should be driving or pushing off your feet at all times. If you are mounted, you apply pressure by driving your hips into your opponent while extending your legs. The same is true for when you have someone's back.

Let's go back and analyze both examples and see what should be the correct approach to maintain the position. In passing the guard, once you have pinned the opponent and reached his side, rather than let go of the legs for the "big leap," you should drive your chest down, pressing against his midsection, and slowly drive your upper body up until you are chest-

20

to-chest, pressing him flat against the mat. At this point, you can let go of the legs, as you have achieved side-control.

In the example of the mount with the choke on, most beginners and even many advanced practitioners have a tendency to focus so much on the submission that they forget that maintaining the position is the main objective. As your opponent bridges to escape, instead of insisting on the choke you should immediately let go of the collar, open your arms, and brace to stop the roll and remain mounted. Once you have maintained the position, you can go back to considering another attack.

Although the general rule is to maintain a position at all costs, at times you need to quickly release a position to advance to another position. The position you find yourself in may be so tight and have so much control that it would take a lot more effort to maintain it and advance than to release and advance. This may be because you are so tight that any movement is difficult, or because you have so much control over your opponent that he gets overly defensive. For example, when you mount him and attack his neck and arms, he may simply choose to keep both arms tight against the body, elbows closed and hands close against the neck. Since defense is always more effective than attacks and involves quicker moves, if we corner an opponent too much, the task of finishing him will be very difficult. In such cases, it is a good idea to do the release-and-advance strategy, giving him a small opening to try to venture out of his shell.

Another example: You are on the bottom, having the opponent in the half-guard. Many times, your leg trapping the opponent's leg is actually preventing you from moving and replacing the guard. Instead, you choose to keep trapping, limiting your own options while the opponent advances to eventually pass. Again, the release-and-advance strategy is the answer.

Movement

Movement is a very important element in Gracie jiu-jitsu. To attain a better position or to escape from a bad position, you need to move your body in relation to your opponent. Generally speaking, being able to move your hips and especially bend at the waist are keys to success. While both may sound simple and trivial, you would be surprised to see, in actual training and fighting situations, how natural it is to do exactly the opposite—to be stiff and remain still. Bending at the waist (jack-knifing or coiling your body) allows you to replace the guard and escape from the mount, and even allows you to sweep. Remember, the body has to work as a unit; your core or hips connect your upper body to your lower body, but it needs to be a flexible connector, not a stiff one. A snake can wrap itself around its prey while a board cannot! For example, it is quite common to see a person trying to escape from the mount using the hip escape while keeping his body completely straight as he pushes against the knee with his arms (as if he is trying to push his body up and through the opponent's legs). The correct way would be to brace with the arms against the knee and bend at the waist as you escape your hips.

Another important thing to remember in movement is that you generally want to move to deflect the power of your opponent, rather than force your way against it. For example, you are passing the guard and your opponent has both hands on your hips, blocking you from reaching his side. Rather than trying to force your weight and body against his arms, you should simply turn your hips and deflect his arms and his power away from your hips, and take side-control. It is important to remember, every time you fight power with power, you are not using technique. You are not using Gracie jiu-jitsu and its wealth of options.

Transitions

Another yardstick of progress is one's ability to transition quickly and smoothly between positions. The ability to transition and flow from one position to another is key to controlling a bigger opponent and advancing in the fight. The science of the sport is based on leverage, action and reaction, and anticipation. While in any martial art transitions are key, in Gracie jiu-jitsu, many of the moves are linked together in combination, and one's ability to flow between them is a great asset. Examples of moves linked together are sweep/submission combos like the armlock and choke from the guard, a scissor sweep/choke from the guard, or an across-side attack that transitions to taking the back. Transitions between positions can be necessary as simple advancements or defensive necessities, such as realizing a position is lost, or they can be done as a setup for other moves, such as a release with a purpose.

Realizing when a position is lost. Many times a novice and even some advanced practitioners fail to recognize when a position is lost. Instead of anticipating the loss of control and moving on to the proper counter or next position in the sequence, they fight to regain an otherwise lost situation, as the opponent advances even more. An example of this is keeping your legs closed to maintain closed guard when the opponent has proper technique and is forcing you to open the guard. Many times fighters will still fight to keep their feet crossed, only wasting their energy and getting discouraged or disappointed when the guard is finally broken. A better option would be, as soon as you realize the control is lost, to open the guard and place a foot on the hips and one on the biceps, or some other open-guard strategy. The energy and time

Slow Down! Royce kicks Akebono, keeping him off his game. K-1 Dynamite, December 31, 2004. Photo courtesy K-1.

wasted fighting for the lost cause simply weakens you. Another example is to bridge and continue bridging to escape the mount, even though your opponent has already braced and effectively blocked that option, rather than simply changing to an elbow escape. Another very common and very frustrating example is when you are mounted, trying for an armlock, and the opponent has already escaped his elbow from your control, but you still try the armlock, only to end up on the bottom with your opponent in your guard. Not only did you lose the submission, but you also lost the great mount position. Now you are on the bottom with your opponent ready to pass your guard. A better option would have been to readjust the grip or look for another attack. Many times in the heat of the battle we lock ourselves into one goal and fight for only that goal. Start to pay attention and begin to realize when a position is lost. The sooner you start to realize the situation, the sooner you will transition to something that works for you.

Releasing pressure with a purpose. As we mentioned earlier, sometimes an advanced practitioner will actually release pressure, encouraging the opponent to escape a certain way, in order to advance his position even more. An example of this is when you are in side-control and you release the pressure of your chest on the opponent's chest so that he turns to his knees, giving you the back. This is a very effective strategy since you are anticipating the escape and setting a trap. In his struggle to escape a bad position, an opponent will immediately react to any opening, doing exactly what you want. The key here is to know the likely escape route, give him enough space that he feels he can escape but not so much that he will sense the danger, and to be able to move quickly and capitalize when he exposes himself. It is no use to set up a trap if you don't know the end result or if you are not quick and agile enough to take advantage of the situation that you created. By using the training methods described above, you will be able to sharpen this strategy and technique.

Combinations. Combinations of moves are the key to success in the art. If Gracie jiu-jitsu is to be a chess match, a person's ability to plan attacks with multiple steps and options is the key to winning the game. Combinations can be defensive or offensive. Examples of a defensive combo are the upa-elbow escape to escape the mount and the bridge-guard replacement to escape from across-side. Attacking combos include the choke-armlock from the guard and the double or triple attack from the mount. The keys to developing combinations are knowledge of the available moves and options, ability to transition between them, and ability to see or feel them and react quickly to an opportunity.

One of the ways to develop combinations is to start with two closely related moves that you can execute instinctively. After mastering their application and execution, try connecting the two together. Once you have mastered the two of them together, look for another move that is closely related and add it to the combination. Using this process of linking moves together, after a while you will have a series of sequences that will be effective and instinctive. As your combinations get more complex, you will start to realize that the moves can link within each other and branch out on their own. For example, you go back to the simple sweep/armlock from the guard. You attempt the sweep and as the opponent posts up to brace, you take the arm, and vice-versa. Then you have the triangle choke–armlock combo, and you may add the omoplata to it, or may find that the original sweep/armlock combo opens up the omoplata option as well, leading to the triangle, and so forth. Start practicing the combinations as described, then let your imagination and creativity link them together.

Visualization

Don't underrate the power of visualization. By visualizing the moves in your mind before a match, you can help condition your mind to reacting in certain ways to certain situations. By "playing" entire sequences of sparring sessions in your mind, you will be able to sharpen your subconscious mind whether you are training or not. Visualization is a very effective way of "practicing" your moves and actually imprinting a mental picture of what a move should "feel" like and when it can be executed. I like to sit in a quiet place and start out by going through one move, and then progress into sequences, and then advance into full sparring visualization. A few days before a fight, I'll take a coach in a room with me, dim the lights, start doing relaxation breathing, and begin to talk. I describe what I see in the fight. We go through the scenarios and options. I see the fight going this way, but if my opponent does this, then we will do that. If he does that, then we will do this, and so forth.

You can visualize fights during your everyday training and at completely different times. Some days you can't practice, but you can still perform these mental exercises to stay mentally sharp. You can also do them to correct a problem that you may have in certain positions or situations. Often, when you are working out or training, you are too busy concentrating on the now to think of correcting or even noticing what you are doing wrong. However, if you have a certain level of ability and understanding, you may be able to see for yourself what your mistake is by visualizing the situation at some other time.

Belt Structure

To round out your knowledge of the foundations of jiu-jitsu, a basic understanding of belt structure is needed.

White belt. A White belt is a total beginner, an empty glass ready to be filled with information. A white belt has so much to learn that he cannot even focus on what the game is about. He has to concentrate on balance and posture, and to learn basic moves and be able to execute them. A white belt generally does not have any concept of a game or putting moves together. White belt is a great stage! Everything is new and fresh and exciting. But it is also a time of frustration. Many of the moves you learn are not easy to repeat and are very different than what your body wants to do, or can do for that matter. The white belt is always eager to train with anyone and is always humble and open-minded to new techniques and new information. This excellent quality should be carried out throughout your career in jiu-jitsu. Many practitioners, as they advance in training, start to develop a fear of losing and also a false sense of knowledge that stops them from accepting instruction and information. We should all remain as eager and open-minded as white belts!

Blue belt. The blue belt has the basic moves down and is beginning to execute them at a certain level, but he is still not understanding what the game is all about. He learns a new move and wants to use it, regardless of what the opponent is doing. He is focused on the immediate result. Blue belts make a lot of mistakes. The moves are not yet ingrained and they don't have complete knowledge of when they need to use the moves. The blue belt has a lot of fun, because he can see his progress from white belt, but he is still prey to most higher belts in the school. The blue belt should concentrate on learning more moves and practicing the moves until they are automatic. When he is in a difficult position, all the blue belt wants to do is escape, without any regard for defense. If he is mounted, he will do an upa or a series of upas, without worrying about his neck or arm and without worrying if the situation calls for an elbow escape instead. His focus is just here and now.

Purple belt. The purple belt has the knowledge of most of the moves that he needs to become a black belt. He is beginning to understand the game and can think a couple of moves ahead. His execution of the moves is much better than the blue belts, but not close to the brown and black belts yet. His timing has improved, but he still always uses direct moves, focused on the objective ahead. The purple belt should concentrate on improving his defensive skills in addition to the overall game. His ego may not let him get himself into difficult positions with lower belts, but that is exactly what he should be doing. By allowing himself to be in difficult positions with lower belts, he will improve his defensive skills and his escapes, and that is one of the most important steps for his advancement to the higher belts. Practicing with lower belts ensures a better chance of succeeding. If a purple belt allows a brown or black belt to take his back, it may be very difficult to escape and he may end up tapping. Purple belt is a fun level, as you have the status of being an advanced belt without the pressure of performing to the black belt level. Much is expected from the purple if he is to reach brown, however. This is the stage in training where you begin to develop your own style and game. The purple is considered the key belt, the belt where many people give up because they can't reach the brown level. The key is to have fun and train hard, while constantly seeking technical knowledge and repetition.

Brown belt. Brown is an elite belt, one step away from the coveted black. The brown belt knows as much as any black belt and has a good understanding of the game, as well as what is required to succeed both in training and competition. Unlike the blue and purple, the brown belt is capable of adjusting his game to fit the opponent. He should be equally capable of passing and defending the guard and have good defensive skills. His moves include more complex sequences and advanced planning. A brown belt typically thinks three to four moves ahead, while the blue only thinks of the immediate move and the purple may think two moves ahead. The brown belt has already selected what moves are best for his own body type, what moves should be a part of his repertoire, and he concentrates on improving his understanding of when, where, and against what kind of opponent they work best. The main difference between the brown belt and black belt is the fact that brown still makes decisional mistakes and still falls for feints with greater regularity than the black. Practice and repetition to improve timing will help him reach the next level.

Black belt. The black belt is attained once an individual has complete understanding of the sport. The black belt should be a leader, a studious individual who not only perfects his own moves but also looks deeper than the surface for the finest details and nuances that improve the effectiveness of each move. At this stage, it is not a matter of learning new moves (although one should never stop learning), but instead how to better the moves. Once you achieve the black belt level, the game becomes more mental. You really have a set game with solid moves that work in most situations, and you execute them perfectly without hesitation. Your understanding of training and defense and attack and submissions is very deep. The journey that got you here was full of detours and challenges, and you passed them all. It is like driving a car: At first you don't know enough and you concentrate on the road, shifting, breaking, and accelerating. You are too busy with the basic functions to worry about the road signs or the radio. That is the blue belt. As you get better, your control of the vehicle is better. You are able to drive and change radio stations, but when you are on the freeway going a little faster, you need someone else to read the signs for you as you cannot take your eyes off the road. That is the purple. As you get a little more practiced, you start to read the signs yourself, you can change the radio and relax behind the wheel. The problem still is that although you can read the signs, they sometimes don't mean anything to you, or by the time you realize what they mean, you already missed the exit. That would be the brown. Once you reach your black belt, you can drive, change radio stations, look at the signs and make your own decision to react to the signs as you see fit to best reach your destination. Detours are nothing more than slightly different routes to the inevitable objective.

MEET THE TEAM

The Authors

Royce Gracie

Royce Gracie shocked the world when he entered the Ultimate Fighting Championship in 1993 as an unknown and defeated much larger opponents in record time. He went on to win two more UFCs and many other events. In doing so, he introduced America to Gracie jiu-jitsu, now the most in-demand martial art in the world. Royce's stamina is legendary. The result of natural ability and his unique training program, it has allowed him to achieve superhuman feats, including being the only person in No-Holds-Barred fighting history to defeat four opponents in a single night, and fighting the longest match in modern No-Holds-Barred history—a 90-minute marathon at the Tokyo Dome in 2002 in front of 90,000 spectators. Royce trains top-level martial artists at his Southern California academy, teaches international seminars, and continues to fight professionally. He is the author of two bestsellers: *Brazilian Jiu-Jitsu Self-Defense Techniques* and *Superfit.*

Kid Peligro

One of the leading martial arts writers in the world, Kid Peligro is responsible for regular columns in *Bodyguard* and *Gracie Magazine*, as well as one of the most widely read Internet MMA news pages, *ADCC News*. He has been the author or coauthor of an unprecedented string of bestsellers in recent years, including *The Gracie Way, Brazilian Jiu-Jitsu: Theory and Technique, Brazilian Jiu-Jitsu Self-Defense Techniques, Brazilian Jiu-Jitsu Black Belt Techniques, Brazilian Jiu-Jitsu Submission Grappling Techniques,* and *Superfit.* A black belt in jiu-jitsu, Kid's broad involvement in the martial arts has led him to travel to the four corners of the Earth as an ambassador for the sport that changed his life. He makes his home in San Diego.

The Advisors

Pedro and Guilherme Valente were born into the Gracie jiu-jitsu tradition. Their father is a seventh-degree black and red belt who holds the title of Master in Gracie Jiu-Jitsu. At age three, Pedro and Gui were already taking private lessons from Grandmaster Helio Gracie. Growing up, the Valente brothers trained daily at the original Gracie Academy in Rio de Janeiro under Helio, Royler, and Rolker Gracie. Pedro started teaching Gracie jiu-jitsu in Miami in the 1990s. With the help of Rorion and Royce Gracie, he founded a jiu-jitsu club at the University of Miami. With his brother Gui, he opened the Gracie Miami Jiu-Jitsu Academy a few years later. The brothers' excellent instructional skills, combined with their technical fighting styles, allowed them to receive their black belts and instructor certificates directly from grandmaster Helio Gracie. The brothers currently own one of the largest and most successful Gracie jiu-jitsu schools in the nation. Furthermore, Pedro holds a masters degree in Business Administration from the University of Miami and Gui holds a degree in Sport Management from Barry University.

CLOSING THE DISTANCE AND CLINCHING

The ability to properly close the distance between you and your opponent in a street fight or an NHB match can be the difference between being able to bring the fight to your element or being out cold. Yet many schools gloss over this vital part of surviving an altercation. They concentrate on dramatic holds and submissions, yet ignore the key part of every fight that precedes these. If you cannot properly close the distance between you and your opponent, you will never get the opportunity to try any submissions. Royce's game has always stood out for its variety of safe and effective ways to close the distance and clinch. Any time you come in for a clinch you run the risk of being hit with the opponent's strike, so it is very important to avoid the "power zone" of your opponent's strike. Always be either too far or too close, never in between. This way the aggressor will never find the adequate distance necessary to deliver a successful strike.

1. Clinching after a jab

A jiu-jitsu specialist will frequently use a punch or kick to close the distance and clinch. In this technique Royce demonstrates both the preferred and incorrect ways of clinching after your opponent throws a jab.

1 Royce stands a safe distance from Pedro and throws a jab, stretching his left arm to gauge his distance from Pedro. Notice that Royce is standing with the same stance as Pedro; his left leg is forward opposite Pedro's left leg. This is very important for this type of clinch.

2 Pedro reacts to Royce's jab by countering with a jab of his own. Royce uses his right hand to deflect Pedro's left jab as he steps forward with his left leg while his head does a semicircle to the outside of Pedro's body. Royce is safe and avoids the strike as his head ducks outside of Pedro's range. Notice that Royce's head ends up behind Pedro's left shoulder. This is extremely important. If his head went toward Pedro's chest, he could be hit with a right punch.

3 ***Alternate stance.*** Royce stands with the opposite leg facing Pedro. Notice that he has his left leg forward while Pedro has his right leg forward.

4 ***Incorrect finish.*** As Royce throws his left jab and steps forward to clinch, the timing needs to be much sharper because of the potential danger of the strike. Otherwise, Royce leaves his face vulnerable to a strike—in this case Pedro's left punch to his face.

2. Takedown after a jab

Technique 1 showed the proper way to clinch after your opponent throws a jab. Here, Royce continues that move to a takedown and mount.

1 As in position 1, Pedro throws a jab and Royce closes the distance and goes for the clinch. He parries the strike with his right hand and takes a step forward with his left leg while circling his head to his own right to avoid the jab. Notice how Royce's arms are open and around Pedro's torso.

2 Royce clinches Pedro by locking his hands together while keeping his head close to Pedro's left shoulder.

2 *Detail* Notice Royce's hands gripping each other with open palms. Also notice how Royce's head is tight against Pedro's left shoulder. This is for two reasons. He doesn't want to give any space for Pedro to bring his left arm around and in front of his face, negating the back control. He also wants to take away Pedro's ability to deliver an elbow to the face.

3 *Detail* Keep your head close to the opponent's back, otherwise he can hit you with an elbow!

3 Royce walks around to Pedro's back. Notice how he continues to press his head against Pedro's back, otherwise he could still fall prey to an elbow strike. Also notice how Royce is still clinching Pedro tightly around the chest.

4 Royce drops his arms to Pedro's waist as he steps back to create some distance. Notice Royce's foot placement in relation to Pedro's: his left foot is near Pedro's left foot while his right foot is away for balance. If his right foot was close to Pedro's right foot, Royce could easily fall back if Pedro stepped back or leaned back.

5 In a quick motion, Royce takes a small step forward with his left foot and places his right foot just behind Pedro's right foot, blocking him from moving back, and bends his left leg as if he wants to sit on his left foot at the same time. Royce pulls Pedro back with his arms, causing Pedro to fall backwards.

6 As Pedro begins to fall, Royce releases his hands and tucks his right elbow in to avoid hitting the ground and to prevent it from being caught under Pedro's body. Royce uses Pedro's downward momentum to pull himself over the top.

7 Royce then loops his left leg over and achieves the mount. Again, notice how Royce keeps his head close to Pedro's left shoulder to block him from turning to his left and having his back flat on the ground.

8 And to keep from being hit by an elbow strike!

3. Hip-throw takedown

The ability to take the fight to the ground, to the element where you have more skill and control than your opponent, is another overlooked technique in many jiu-jitsu schools. With the ever increasing focus on tournament fighting with rules and restrictions, many practitioners ignore these techniques and concentrate on techniques that work once the fight hits the ground. But in real life, things may work differently and your opponent will not be so eager to go to the ground with you. It is important for the martial artist who wants to learn not only how to win tournaments but also how to survive real-life situations to learn different clinching and takedown techniques from various situations. Royce believes that the primary function of a martial art is to teach the practitioner to defend himself from a "real life" confrontation. In this technique, Royce takes advantage of Pedro's punch with his back hand to clinch. A full punch travels a longer distance than a jab, giving Royce enough time to quickly step in and block it.

1 Royce and Pedro are facing each other with a square stance, both with the same (left) leg forward.

2 As Pedro initiates his punch, Royce quickly drops his weight down and starts to lean forward. Notice how Royce has his guard up, with both arms slightly bent and his fists protecting his face from strikes.

3 Royce steps forward with his left leg and drives his head toward Pedro's chest. Notice Royce still has his guard up, protecting his face.

4 Royce intercepts Pedro's right punch with his left hand and clinches Pedro. He grabs Pedro's left arm with his right hand as well, blocking him from throwing a left punch.

4 **Detail** Notice how Royce cups Pedro's arm with his hand, gripping behind the triceps. This ensures that Pedro cannot pull the arm back and cock it for another punch. It also keeps Royce in close proximity and in control of Pedro's upper body.

5 In firm control of Pedro, Royce steps around to his right until his hips are perpendicular to Pedro's hips. Notice that Royce has his feet at equal distance to each side of Pedro's body to maintain balance and control as Pedro struggles to escape. Royce retains control of Pedro's right arm with his left hand and slides his right arm around Pedro's back, cupping the right hand on the right hip.

6 Royce steps in front of Pedro with his right foot, planting it between Pedro's feet.

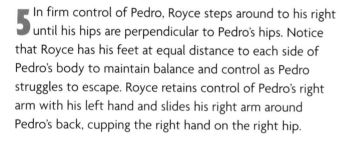

7 Royce squares his hips in front of Pedro's hips by stepping in with his left foot. He wants to make sure of two things: first, that his feet are square and inside of Pedro's feet; second, that his hip is square in front of Pedro's hips, slightly out to the right to prevent Pedro from sliding down as he prepares the hip throw. Royce bends his knees, lowering his hips and locking them with Pedro's hips, and begins the throw by bending at the waist as he drops his head forward while pulling Pedro's right arm across his body with his left hand.

8 As Royce drops his head and extends his legs, he launches Pedro up in the air in a nasty throw.

9 Pedro ends up on the ground with Royce in firm control, still holding Pedro's right arm with his left hand. Royce's right knee is near Pedro's right ribcage. From here, Royce can execute an armlock, drop to knee-on-stomach position and rain punches on Pedro, or simply get side-control.

4. Counter to hip-throw defense 1: opponent straightens his body

In this situation Royce has achieved the clinch and wants to use the hip throw to get Pedro on the ground, as in technique 3. But Pedro straightens his body, making a stiff hip and preventing Royce from coming in with his hips for the hip throw. Royce takes advantage of Pedro's reaction and uses this takedown.

1 Royce has clinched Pedro and is in perfect position for a hip throw. His hips are 90 degrees from Pedro's and his arms are wrapped around Pedro's waist. Royce has his feet in base and can follow Pedro should he try to pull away. Pedro senses the hip throw, straightens his body, and pushes his hips forward slightly, making it difficult for Royce to step in front with his right leg and square his hips.

2 Royce cinches his arm grip around Pedro's waist and drops his body down, bending his knees.

3 Royce extends his legs as he drives his hips into Pedro's hips and lifts Pedro off the ground. Note that Royce uses his legs and hips, not his arms and back, to lift Pedro off the ground. The legs and hips can generate much more explosive power and are less likely to be injured than the back.

4 With Pedro in the air, Royce dips his right shoulder, twisting Pedro.

5 To complete the takedown, Royce drives Pedro to the ground. Notice that a throw like this can quickly end a fight as Pedro would be piledriven into the concrete with Royce's weight and force driving him in.

5. Counter to hip-throw defense 2: opponent drops and tries to pull away

Continuing with the possible counters to the hip escape, in this case Pedro drops down in base, leans away from Royce, and tries to pull away from the control. Royce takes advantage of Pedro's reaction and the fact that he is leaning away to apply this trip takedown.

1 Royce has positioned himself for a hip throw. He has control of Pedro's right arm with his left, his right arm is wrapped around Pedro's back and holding Pedro's right hip, and his body is 90 degrees from Pedro's, ready to execute the hip throw.

2 Pedro counters the hip throw by dropping down in base, leaning to his right, and putting his weight on his right leg as he tries to pull away from Royce.

3 Sensing that Pedro's weight is on the right leg and off the left, Royce hooks Pedro's left leg with his right one and pulls it back, twisting Pedro to the right.

4 This Forces Pedro to spin counterclockwise, losing his balance and falling to the mat.

5 ***Reverse angle*** From this angle we can see how Royce undercuts Pedro's balance.

6 Continuing with the reverse angle, we see that Pedro falls to the mat and Royce follows him. Royce plants his arms on each side of Pedro's body and drops his left knee over Pedro's right leg, leaving his foot hooked.

7 Royce mounts Pedro.

6. Takedown from the clinch 1: push-and-pull

In this situation Royce has already trapped Pedro's arms. Perhaps Pedro threw a sucker punch or a back punch or they just ended up this way during a scramble. It's good to have more than one alternative in your arsenal to take the fight to the ground, otherwise you can become too predictable. Some people find this takedown more suitable to their style, while others find the previous ones preferable, but they are equally effective.

1 Royce has clinched Pedro and has control of Pedro's arms with his hands gripping the triceps.

2 As Pedro tries to pull away, Royce quickly drops down and drops his arms, locking them around Pedro's waist, clasping his hands tight while driving his head into Pedro's chest.

3 Royce breaks Pedro's posture as he straightens his legs and continues to drive his head forward, pushing on Pedro's chest. At the same time, he pulls his arms in, driving Pedro's hips in. Notice how this action of pushing at the top and pulling at the bottom causes Pedro to bend back and lose his balance.

4 Royce continues to walk forward, still gripping Pedro's waist tight as Pedro falls to the ground.

5 Royce lets go and braces with his arms so he doesn't hit his face on the ground. He ends up mounted on Pedro.

7. Takedown from the clinch 2: trip

In this situation, Royce has a similar clinch to the one he used in technique 6, but Pedro maintains a better posture, doing a slight sprawl to keep Royce from bending him as in the previous technique. Since Pedro stands very erect, Royce uses Pedro's reaction and lack of base to accomplish a tripping takedown.

1 Royce has clinched Pedro. His arms are wrapped around Pedro's body, hands clasped together. Pedro is very erect and prevents Royce from bending his body back.

2 Royce steps forward with his right leg and loops it around Pedro's left leg.

3 Royce drives his head forward on Pedro's chest and uses his right leg to pull Pedro's left leg out toward the right, causing Pedro to fall back to the ground. Notice that Pedro does not fall straight back but rather to Royce's right because his leg is being pulled.

4 Royce follows Pedro to the ground and ends up on top.

8. Side-kick

The side-kick is one of the most effective moves in jiu-jitsu. The quickness of the motion and the pain of a strike to the thigh just above the knee will stop most opponents from coming in. It can be even more devastating when directed against the knee itself, often causing it to buckle. This move is an effective way to maintain distance from your opponent's strikes, but can also be used as a prelude to a clinch. Notice that the motion is short and snappy as Royce quickly coils his leg and snaps it on Pedro's thigh. Also notice that Royce puts the weight of his body behind the strike, otherwise a strong opponent may drive forward and throw Royce off-balance. Also notice that Pedro does not have the space to hit Royce with either a punch or a kick.

1 Royce stands in front of Pedro with his left arm out to gauge his distance.

2 Royce lifts his left leg and brings his foot back.

3 Royce coils his left foot all the way to his right leg . . .

4 And snaps his leg forward, side-kicking Pedro's left thigh.

4 *Detail* Notice how Royce curls his toes so they don't get caught in Pedro's pants, which could break them. This also ensures that Royce strikes Pedro's thigh with the bottom center of his foot, making solid contact. He doesn't want to strike with the heel or the ball of the foot, which could slide past the thigh.

9. Clinching from the side-kick

Royce loves the side-kick. A good side-kick not only prevents the opponent from coming forward, but also can be a great setup for the clinch. An opponent will usually react to a side-kick by leaning back or stepping back to avoid the strike. This is the best time to clinch; with the opponent retreating, he has no power for a strike of his own.

1 Royce throws an offensive side-kick, striking Pedro's left thigh with his left foot. Pedro leans back to absorb the power. In such a position, he won't have any power behind his strikes.

2 Royce takes advantage of this and lunges forward for the clinch. He takes a big step forward with his left leg, closing the distance and clinching Pedro. Notice how Royce cleverly uses his right hand to push Pedro's left arm out of the way so he can clinch and quickly go to Pedro's back.

3 Royce wraps his arms around Pedro's waist to control him and takes a step forward with his right leg to get to Pedro's back. Note Royce's head position—up close to Pedro's back to protect him from any elbow strikes that Pedro may attempt.

4 Royce uses the same movements as in technique 4 to lift Pedro off the ground and execute a takedown.

10. Hip-throw counter

To develop a complete game, it's important to learn not just how to do a hip throw but how to counter one as well. As Pedro positions himself for the hip throw, Royce reacts by dropping his weight to counter the action and follows through, using his weight to drive Pedro down to the ground.

1 Pedro is in good position for a hip throw. He may have used this as a counter to the back clinch or may be simply executing a hip throw. He controls Royce's left arm with his right hand and grabs Royce's belt with his left one. His hips are squared with Royce, ready to execute the throw.

2 The moment Pedro dips down to start the throw, Royce drops his weight on top of Pedro's left (throwing) leg. Notice how Royce hangs his weight down by bending his right knee and pushing off his left leg.

3 Royce continues to force his weight on top of Pedro's left leg as he now drops his left shoulder down and twists his arms, forcing Pedro to lose his balance.

4 Pedro drops to the ground with Royce in control of him. Royce's arms are tightly clasped around Pedro's waist, his right leg remains bent with the knee up, and his left knee is on the ground. Royce's head pushes against Pedro's back, protecting from an elbow strike and pressing Pedro down as well.

5 As soon as he has Pedro completely down on the ground, Royce spreads his left leg out, planting the foot wide to keep base and to control Pedro. From here Royce can quickly move from side to side or deliver knee strikes to Pedro's side.

11. Kimura counter to a rear clinch 1

Having someone clinching you from the back is a situation that should be avoided at all costs. As Royce has demonstrated in previous techniques, the opponent has many options for takedowns. This situation occasionally occurs, however, because of your opponent's quick decision or a mistake on your part, so you should have a counter at hand. Royce likes to use the Kimura in such situations.

1 Pedro has achieved a rear clinch on Royce. His arms are wrapped around Royce's waist, hands clasped together ready for a takedown. Royce immediately reacts by grabbing Pedro's right wrist with his left hand and prying it out slightly to make space for Royce's right hand to come in. Notice Royce's right hand is straight like a knife in preparation for slicing between Pedro's right arm and Royce's own right thigh.

2 Royce leans to his left to create more space and slides his right hand between his thigh and Pedro's right arm, making sure his arm wraps above Pedro's elbow to lock in the arm.

3 Royce locks his right hands to his left wrist, having achieved the proper control over the arm to execute the Kimura lock.

3 *Detail* Notice Royce's left hand locked around Pedro's right wrist and his right hand locked onto his own left wrist. In both cases Royce has his thumb open, gripping around the wrist for maximum control and keeping Pedro from yanking or jerking his wrist out.

4 Royce steps forward and to his right with his left leg.

5 Royce Leans back and hooks his right foot inside Pedro's right leg, leaving his knee out next to Pedro's right hip.

6 Royce squats down on his left leg, pulling Pedro to the ground with him. Royce makes sure to keep his right-foot-hook pressure against Pedro's leg to prevent him from coming around to the side.

7 As Royce reaches the ground, he loops his left leg over Pedro's right leg, preventing him from rolling over his right shoulder to escape the Kimura.

8 Royce escapes his hips to his left, turning his body toward Pedro as he drops his right knee down and in front of Pedro's hips, and lifts Pedro's right wrist toward the right ear, applying torque to the right shoulder.

8 **Detail** Notice Royce's lock on Pedro's arm and the direction of the crank of the arm toward Pedro's right ear.

12. Kimura counter to a rear clinch 2: opponent defends

Sometimes a skilled opponent will successfully defend the Kimura in technique 11, perhaps because both fighters are sweaty or because he is strong. Regardless, it is important to have another option ready so you don't end up cornered without a counter. A natural move is to place the opponent in the guard. In effect, even if you fail the submission, you begin with your attacker clinched on your back and you end up with him in your guard—a much better position than when you started.

1 Royce has Pedro in a Kimura lock and is ready to crank the shoulder.

2 Pedro somehow is able to pry his arm out of Royce's control. Royce then pushes off his left foot and slides his hips away from Pedro and to his right, getting them centered with Pedro's hips. It is very important for Royce to slide his hips back away from Pedro, otherwise Pedro has the closeness for the guard pass. Remember that in general a defender wants distance from his opponent when his guard is open and closeness when his guard is closed. Also notice that Royce remains in control of Pedro's right wrist with his left hand, thus preventing Pedro from grabbing under Royce's armpit or around his neck. Should Pedro be able to do so, he would have a lot more control over Royce and would have the elements to pass the guard.

3 While still controlling Pedro's right wrist, Royce loops his right leg around Pedro's left leg . . .

4 Until he has his knee near Pedro's left hip.

5 Royce then raises his left leg and locks his feet behind Pedro's back, achieving the guard position.

13. Takedown from the front clinch: inside trip

A great option for a takedown from the front clinch is the inside trip. When you achieve a front clinch, the normal reaction of your opponent is to struggle and try to pry himself away from you. This is the perfect time to go for the inside trip. His momentum is already going away and you just give him the additional incentive to fall in that direction.

1 Royce has clinched Pedro. His head is pressing against Pedro's chest and his arms are locked around Pedro's torso.

2 Pedro struggles to escape as he steps to his left.

3 Royce loops his right leg in and around Pedro's left leg and kicks it back, tripping him. Simultaneously, Royce leans forward and pushes his head against Pedro's chest.

4 Without the left leg to brace and with Royce pushing forward on his chest with his head, Pedro falls down. Royce releases his handgrip and uses his hands to brace his fall.

5 Notice that as Pedro's back hits the ground, Royce ends up on top with his shins pushing on Pedro's thighs and knees above them, ready to go for the mount!

14. Front-clinch knee strike

Many times when faced with a front clinch, the opponent will try to back away or sprawl to prevent a takedown. This is the perfect time for a knee strike to the belly.

1 Royce has a front clinch on Pedro.

2 Pedro tries to pull away and keep Royce from further cinching his arm grip around the waist by driving his hips back. Royce steps back with his right leg and prepares for the knee strike.

3 Pushing off his right foot, Royce drives his right knee up toward Pedro's stomach.

4 Royce drives his knee strike into Pedro's stomach. The secret of a good strike is to drive the power through the target instead of aiming to stop at the target. Royce drives his knee as if he wants it to go through Pedro's body for full power.

15. Double-leg takedown

The ability to clinch and take the opponent to the ground is essential. Once there your jiu-jitsu techniques should give you a great advantage over a lesser opponent. In this sequence Royce demonstrates one of his favorite takedowns, the double-leg. Royce typically likes to precede a clinch with a strike, to throw his opponent off guard, so in this case he throws a left jab to Pedro's face and follows it with the takedown. It is very important to make sure that you are in a square stance with your opponent (same leg forward) before you go for the double-leg take-down, otherwise you leave your face open to a knee strike or an uppercut, as Royce will demonstrate at the end of this technique.

1 Royce faces Pedro with a square stance and with his left leg forward. He steps forward with his left leg and throws a left-hand jab to Pedro's face.

2 Pedro's natural reaction is to concentrate on the top strike, so Royce squats forward on his left knee between Pedro's legs and drags his right knee as if he was doing a forward lunge. Notice Royce opened his arms slightly wider than Pedro's legs and reached with his hands to grab the thighs.

3 As soon as he grabs Pedro's legs, Royce continues to drag his right knee forward until it is in line with his left knee. Notice where Royce's knees are in relation to Pedro's feet. Since they had their left legs forward, Royce followed the left jab with his left leg, so his left knee is between Pedro's legs and his right one is to the right of Pedro's left leg. His knees are lined up with Pedro's feet, his left shoulder pushes against Pedro's left hip, and his hands are behind Pedro's knees.

4 Royce continues to drive his left knee forward, sliding it between Pedro's legs while driving his shoulder against Pedro's hips and pulling the knees with his arms to prevent Pedro from taking a step back to regain his balance.

5 Since it is impossible for him to step back, Pedro falls.

6 Pedro ends up on the ground with Royce on top ready to pass the guard.

7 Incorrect way Notice that if Royce comes in for the clinch with an open stance (opposite leg forward), he leaves his face open for a knee strike or a punch.

16. Dropping for the double-leg takedown

Don't forget that Gracie jiu-jitsu techniques are meant to work on the streets as well as on the mat. A simple technique like the clinch lunge when done incorrectly may not have serious consequences on the soft mats that you practice on, but may lead to a broken kneecap on the streets. Royce wants your techniques to work equally well on the mats and on the streets, so he demonstrates the correct and incorrect ways to lunge for the clinch.

Incorrect

1 Royce has his left leg forward and is ready to lunge for the clinch.

2 Royce starts to lean forward . . .

3 And drops his left knee on the mat (leading to an injured kneecap).

Correct

1 Royce has his left leg forward and is ready to lunge for the clinch.

2 Royce takes a big step forward with his left leg, planting his left foot on the ground. Notice that his left knee is up and he drags his right knee.

3 Royce continues to lean forward and begins to lower his left knee to the mat.

4 Royce has both knees on the mat. Notice that at no time in this sequence does Royce drop down to the knee. Instead, he gently lands under control by leaning forward until his left knee touches the ground. This controlled descent works on any surface without injuring the knee.

17. Passing the guard after a double-leg takedown 1: mount

Getting an opponent to the ground is a great way to start a match, but once you get there you need to be ready to progress to better positions. Many times after a successful takedown you will find yourself either in the opponent's guard or half-guard. In the case of the double-leg takedown, quick reaction and the use of the right technique will get you far. Rather than waiting for the opponent to close the guard, Royce takes advantage of the moment and immediately goes to work on passing as soon as his opponent hits the mat. Note that this technique works best when your opponent's knee is closed in. If his knee is open, technique 18 is more effective.

1 Royce successfully takes Pedro down with a double-leg takedown. Since he lunged with his left leg forward, Royce will naturally try to pass to his right. Royce controls Pedro's left leg with his right arm. His left knee is placed between Pedro's legs near the coccyx and his right leg is extended.

2 Since Pedro's knee is turned in (from 90 degrees to the ground), Royce goes for the mount. With his right hand, Royce pushes Pedro's left knee in as he steps over it with his right leg. It is not necessary for Royce to completely push the knee in, but rather just brace it and keep it from opening up as he steps over the leg.

3 Royce advances his torso forward, driving his shoulder on Pedro's chest to keep him pinned to the mat.

4 Should Pedro fail to lock the half-guard on Royce's left leg (likely if your opponent is a beginner or a street fighter), Royce will loop his left leg over Pedro's right leg and achieve the mount.

4 *Reverse* Here we see the move from the other side.

18. Passing the guard after a double-leg takedown 2: side-control

This situation is identical to technique 17 except Pedro now has his knee open in relation to the ground. In this case Royce demonstrates an option to go to side-control from the guard pass instead of the mount. This is totally up to you. Some people like to go directly to the mount while others prefer to achieve side-control first.

1 Since Pedro's knee is open (from 90 degrees to the ground), Royce pins Pedro's left leg to the ground with his right hand, pushing down on the left knee.

2 Royce pushes open Pedro's leg, pressing down on the thigh with his right hand, and steps over it with his right leg, bringing his right knee close to Pedro's left side.

3 Dealing with an unskilled fighter who does not close the half-guard, Royce changes his right hand from Pedro's left thigh to under the neck for greater positional control.

4 Royce steps over with his left leg until he reaches side-control.

5 Notice Royce's side-control position. His left knee is bent and almost under Pedro's left leg, making it very difficult for Pedro to replace the guard. His right leg is open for balance and to add pressure to Pedro's chest. Royce's left elbow is tight against Pedro's right hip, virtually locking Pedro's hips between his right elbow and left thigh. And finally, Royce's right arm is wrapped under Pedro's head with the shoulder pushing against the side of the face, keeping Pedro's head straight. Pedro cannot turn to his left to replace the guard without turning his head as well. This is a very important detail!

6 Alternatively, Royce may choose a different side-control stance. Again, this is completely optional; some people feel more control in one or the other. In this case, Royce's right elbow is locked tight against Pedro's right ear to prevent the head from moving; his left hand is placed on the ground next to Pedro's left hip to prevent him from turning to his left, sliding his left knee under Royce's right leg, and replacing the guard.

19. Double-leg takedown 2: opponent leans forward

When faced with a low clinch and the possibility of a double-leg takedown, your opponent may counter by leaning over you. Royce's game is predicated on action-reaction, so rather than fight to force the takedown, Royce takes advantage of Pedro's reaction and goes for an alternative throw. Since Pedro is leaning forward, he is light on his legs; Royce can pick him up and take him down.

1 Royce has a low clinch and is ready for the double-leg takedown. Notice his knees are perfectly placed in relation to Pedro's feet and his hands are blocking Pedro's knees.

2 Sensing an imminent takedown, Pedro immediately counters by leaning forward. At this point Pedro's weight is over Royce's shoulder, making his legs very light.

3 Royce extends his body and lifts Pedro's legs off the ground. This is quite easy since Pedro's head and torso act as counterbalance.

4 Royce dips his left shoulder as he twists Pedro in the air . . .

5 And drops him to the ground. Royce ends up in side-control.

20. Double-leg takedown 3: opponent steps back

Many times when attempting the double-leg takedown, your opponent will step back with one leg and get into base, making it very hard to execute the double-leg takedown. When that happens, a tripping takedown is called for. Again Royce uses Pedro's reaction to determine which technique is best suited for the job.

1 Royce lunges at Pedro, attempting a double-leg takedown. Pedro reacts to the shoot and steps back with his right leg to gain balance.

2 Sensing the counter, Royce does not push for the original takedown but changes to an outside trip. Since Pedro stepped back with his right leg, Royce attacks Pedro's left one (the one in front). While still clinching Pedro, hands gripping behind the knees to prevent him from further stepping away, Royce circles his right leg around, hooking it behind Pedro's left ankle.

3 Notice that Royce traps Pedro's left ankle with his right leg, locking it in the back of his knee.

4 Royce continues to circle his right leg, pulling Pedro's foot off the ground for the trip. At the same time, Royce drives his body forward and down on Pedro's left thigh, forcing Pedro to lose his balance.

5 With nothing to brace on, Pedro has no option but to fall. Notice that Pedro does not fall straight back but rather toward his left because of Royce's pressure to that side.

21. Double-leg takedown 4: opponent sprawls

This time when faced with a double-leg takedown, Pedro opts for a great defense, the sprawl. Reacting quickly to Royce's shoot, Pedro sprawls very far, making it impossible for Royce to execute the takedown. However, Royce looks at Pedro's reaction and sees that Pedro has left a clear path to the back, which Royce takes advantage of.

1 Royce shot in for the double-leg takedown, but Pedro quickly reacted with a solid sprawl. Notice how Pedro thrusts his hips forward and his legs straight back, pushing his belly against Royce's shoulder, making it virtually impossible for Royce to achieve the necessary leverage for the takedown. Also notice how Royce's head is under and behind Pedro's left arm, exposing a clear path to the back.

2 Royce takes a big step forward with his right leg, planting his foot near Pedro's left. He also flings his head back, driving Pedro's left shoulder forward. Notice how Royce's head is tight against Pedro's side, thus preventing Pedro from looping his arm in front of Royce's face to block the move.

3 Pushing off his right leg, Royce stands up, making sure he keeps pressure with his head on Pedro's back. At this point Royce's right arm has come up from the back of Pedro's knee to his right hip, where it locks with the left hand. Notice how Royce clasps his palms together for maximum control of the position, as Pedro will certainly try to struggle away from it.

22. Double forward trip

At times during stand-up action, your opponent has good base and keeps your attempts at taking him off balance at bay. If he feels that his opponent has a very good stand-up game or he simply does not want to waste time getting the fight to his element, Royce will use the double trip to bring the fight to the ground and get his opponent in his guard.

1 Royce and Pedro are fighting for a takedown. Pedro has very good stand-up skills and Royce doesn't want to take any chances getting the fight to his terms.

2 Royce steps with his left foot on top of Pedro's right foot and his right foot on Pedro's left one, locking them in place with his bodyweight.

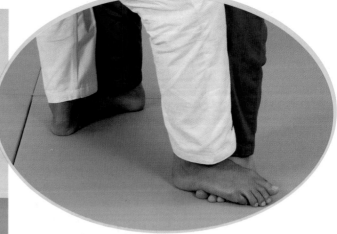

2 *Detail* Notice how Royce steps sideways across the top of Pedro's foot with his feet. This allows greater control because he is able to put the entire weight of his body on Pedro's feet, locking them to the ground. Should Royce simply step straight over Pedro's feet, he wouldn't have the necessary weight on the foot, making it easy for Pedro to simply pull away.

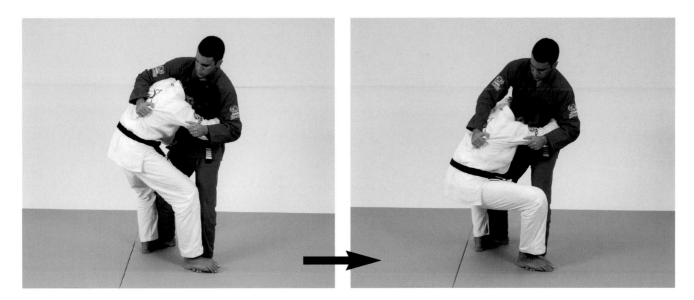

3 With Pedro's feet locked in place, Royce starts to sit back to the ground as he pulls Pedro's body with his arms. Since Pedro cannot step forward, he isn't able to resist Royce's weight pulling him forward, and follows down to the ground.

4 As Pedro starts to fall, Royce releases the pressure on Pedro's foot and opens his legs, forcing Pedro to fall in his guard.

5 Royce locks his legs behind Pedro's back for the closed guard. Notice how Royce's hands lock behind Pedro's triceps with his forearms blocking the biceps for full control. This prevents Pedro from pulling his arm back to deliver a punch. It also prevents Pedro from getting up in posture in preparation for passing Royce's guard.

CLINCHING DRILLS

For most people, facing punches and kicks takes some getting used to. It is not a natural instinct to try to come into a punch or a kick; people often will flinch or close their eyes when a strike is directed at them. Since closing the distance and clinching is perhaps the most dangerous moment in a fight, the ability to calmly see the punches, time them, and learn about critical striking distance is vital. Royce has designed the following sequence of drills to get a person used to closing the gap against an opponent. Remember that repetition is the best way to improve timing and execution, especially for novices. Repeat these drills at least ten times per workout to get the proper mechanics and timing.

23. Clinching drill 1: closing the distance

The first drill deals with clinching through a series of straight punches to the face. Notice that Royce first gets used to the sight of punches coming at him, then notes the range of the punches and how far he can stay before he gets hit. He also notes the timing of the punches so he can come in without catching a punch at full power. As previously stated, the clincher needs to always be either too far or too close, never in between. This way the aggressor will never find the adequate distance necessary to deliver a successful strike.

1 Royce stands in front of Gui, while Gui throws straight punches at his face.

2 Royce lets Gui throw a few punches. He times them and notes the safe distance where the punches end. This is extremely important as it determines where Royce will start his shoot for the clinch. Notice that Royce is safe when he is either too far for Gui's fists to hit him or too close for the punches to generate real power. The ability to safely clear the danger zone in the middle is the difference between a knock-out and a safe clinch.

3 ***For the high clinch:*** Having timed the punches and noted the range, Royce shoots in after Gui's left punch has passed its power zone. Royce can come in then or when the punch has not yet developed, but it is easier to see the punch exhausting its power and follow it back into the attacker's body. Royce takes one big step forward with his front (left) leg while his right hand parries Gui's arm. Notice that Royce shoots under the punch in case his timing or range is a little off.

4 ***For the low clinch:*** Royce takes a deep lunge with his left leg, making sure he keeps his hands in front of him and his forearms blocking his body from any knee strikes that might come.

24. Clinching drill 2: closing and striking

This drill practices the high clinch through straight punches. Royce uses his elbows to deliver strikes and to protect himself from elbow strikes thrown by Gui.

1 Royce closes the gap for a high clinch after timing Gui's punches. He uses the same motion as technique 23. This time, however, he uses his right hand to deflect Gui's punch upwards and comes in with a left elbow strike of his own.

2 As Royce gets close, the power range for Gui's punches is neutralized, but up close elbow strikes are a concern, so Royce lifts his right elbow to block any left elbow strikes that may follow.

3 Having protected his face from Gui's strikes, Royce drops his torso, opens his arms, and clinches Gui.

25. Clinching drill 3: measuring distance

Measuring the distance for strikes is a very important skill to have in order to properly clinch your opponent. In this particular drill, Royce stands in front of Gui while Gui throws a variety of punches. This no-contact drill accomplishes three things at once: It lets you get comfortable having punches thrown at you, gets you used to seeing the punches as they are launched, and teaches you the proper distance each strike requires to make contact. Notice that each strike has a different power range: The jab's power is at the full extension of the arm, the uppercut is at the halfway point with the arm bent, and the elbow strike is a short-range attack. Different strikes also have different speeds in developing.

1 Royce and Gui face each other in a square stance.

2 Gui starts throwing different punches at Royce, such as jabs, elbow strikes . . .

3 Crosses, uppercuts, etc. Royce remains in front, timing them and learning the distance where each is effective.

26. Clinching drill 4: ducking under punches

Having establish the concept of distance and timing in the previous drill, Royce now reacts at contact. This is a great way to perfect timing, as Royce drops and shoots on contact.

1 Royce and Gui face each other in a square stance.

2 Gui throws a left cross and Royce reaches with his left hand and touches the top of Gui's left wrist. At this point, Royce has measured the distance and senses the timing of Gui's punches.

3 Immediately after contact with Gui's hand, Royce ducks under Gui's punches, bending the knees and lunging forward by taking a step with his left leg. Notice that Royce's hands are up and forearm is bent to protect his face.

27. Cinching drill 5: bobbing and weaving

Continuing with the fighting drills, Royce now does the bob and weave as he stands near Gui, ducks under punches, and comes up as the punches go by. This drill is great for developing timing to avoid punches and to come up for a strike of your own.

1 Starting very close to Gui—inside the power range of a cross punch—Royce ducks as Gui throws a right cross. You can vary the strikes you use in this drill with jabs, straight punches, elbows, etc.

2 Royce continues the drill by raising his body between punches. As Gui's right cross goes by, he pops up.

3 Gui then follows with a left cross and Royce again ducks under.

4 Royce continues to duck under.

28. Clinching drill 6: side-kick

The side-kick is a very effective way to maintain distance and keep your opponent from reaching the proper range to deliver any strike. In this case, Royce is avoiding slaps, but they could just as well be other strikes. Whether it is a front kick or a rear kick, he learns to see them developing, times them, and uses the side-kick to block them.

1 Royce and Gui face each other in a square stance. Royce already has his left leg up, ready to deliver a side-kick. As Gui comes forward with a series of slaps, Royce alternates striking Gui's legs and torso with the defensive side-kick.

2 Hold your hands behind your back for a more advanced drill. You'll develop balance as well. Note that if you are off-balance, the side-kick will have no power.

29. Clinching drill 7: kick counter

Kicks are very powerful strikes; the leg is a much heavier limb than the arm and the damage it can deliver is much greater. Since legs are longer than arms, the blows take longer to develop and are easier to see, time, and counter. Royce demonstrates a series of side-kick counters to various kicks. The drill consists of having your partner slowly deliver different kicks while you use the defensive side-kick to keep the distance and to block your partner's ability to strike you. As in all the drills, begin slowly and get the feel for the action. Concentrate on seeing the strike develop and sensing the body language of your partner before he begins the kicking motion. Notice cues that may help you foresee the actual kick coming, such as your partner flinching his arms before he starts to kick. In addition, learn the proper balance you need to effectively deliver the side-kick without falling. Notice that Royce has his weight going forward slightly on all the side-kicks for two reasons: one, to maintain his balance as he strikes the opponent; and two, to add his weight to the kick.

1 Gui prepares a side-kick with his right leg. As he cocks the leg to strike, Royce extends his left leg, striking Gui's left thigh with a side-kick just above the knee. Note that in a self-defense situation Royce could easily hit Gui's knee joint with devastating effects. For drill purposes, strike above the knee only.

2 As Gui prepares to deliver the strike, Royce side-kicks with his left foot aimed at the hip to keep the distance.

3 As Gui begins to deliver the rear kick with his left leg, Royce side-kicks with his left leg at Gui's right thigh.

4 Another option for Royce is to side-kick the hip.

5 Royce delivers a front side-kick to intercept and counter Gui's kick. Notice that Royce aims his kick for the inside of the thigh.

30. Clinching drill 8: combination

Now Royce combines the entire repertoire of drills, using the side-kick to keep Gui at bay and following up with clinches. This is the ultimate drill for clinching. After you have mastered the other drills and clinches, you should have your partner simulate strikes without you knowing which strike he will use and in which combination. Begin slowly; speed is a consequence of proper repetition. After you are comfortable and effective with one speed, have your partner increase the speed. In the beginning, you may start the drill with a limit of which strikes your partner can use. As you master the counter, expand your partner's options. Pay attention to which strikes give you the most trouble and work harder on those drills. Royce only demonstrates a few of the options here, but you can combine all the drills above and all the different strikes.

1 Royce throws an offensive side-kick at Gui's left thigh . . .

2 And follows it with a clinch.

3 Gui delivers a left cross.

4 Royce parries the punch with his left hand as he ducks under and shoots in for the clinch.

5 Royce checks Gui's distance with his left-leg side-kick . . .

6 And shoots in under the right cross.

7 Royce parries Gui's left jab and delivers an inside thigh kick with his left leg.

8 Royce throws a side-kick with his left leg, forcing Gui to lean back . . .

9 And shoots in for the clinch.

PASSING THE GUARD

In Gracie jiu-jitsu it seems that you spend half your time either defending the guard or passing the guard. The importance of proper posture and avoiding submissions and sweeps from the guard cannot be overemphasized. If you cannot have proper posture and avoid the defender's attacks, you are not going to be able to survive in a street fight or a jiu-jitsu match. But surviving alone will not accomplish anything except buy you time; you must be able to pass the guard to be a successful attacker!

To be successful at passing someone's guard, you must first be able to avoid any of the opponent's attacks such as submissions and sweeps. To do that you must have patience and always look for the proper posture before you begin to pass. Second, along the way, if at any time you feel in danger or that something is out of place, it is better to return to a safe point and start over than to simply proceed and fall for an attack. Third, to pass the guard, you must remove all the obstacles that are thrown in your way by the defender, such as stiff arms, legs, or knees. Fourth, you generally need to control the opponent's hip movement and legs. If you are successful at these you should be able to safely and effectively pass the guard.

This section examines the element of posture and demonstrates examples of guard passes and ways to regain the posture.

Proper Posture Before Passing the Guard

If you do not have proper posture in the guard and do not find a position where everything is in place before you attempt to pass the guard, you are subject to reversals or, worse, submissions. A skilled opponent will take advantage of every mistake you make, especially in the closed-guard posture, and will make your mission of passing the guard a veritable minefield. For these reasons, let's first look at some elements that are necessary before you can successfully pass the guard.

Note five things about Royce's posture in Gui's guard. 1. His back is straight with the head held high and the left shoulder slightly back. 2. His eyes are looking straight ahead. 3. His right hand grips Gui's collars together at the sternum level and the left hand grips the belt at waist level. 4. His hips are forward and knees are bent and slightly outside of Gui's hips. 5. He sits on top of his heels.

By keeping his back straight, Royce accomplishes a few things. He keeps his neck as far as possible from Gui's hands, making it difficult for Gui to apply a choke. This also makes it difficult for Gui to pull Royce forward by the collar and break his posture. The head held high adds to the structure of the position. Should Royce let his head down, he'd break the perfect line between the spine and the top of the head, making it much easier for Gui to pull the head down and break the posture. One of the secrets of the posture is keeping this perfect alignment between the spine and the head. You should envision your body being pulled by a string attached to the back of your neck. With every movement to open the opponent's guard, make sure you lead with the string pulling the neck back and keeping your head and back in a straight line.

Since he has his right arm pressing against Gui's chest, Royce's shoulders are not square; rather, his left shoulder is slightly back in relation to his right one. That way Royce further hinders Gui's ability to grab the left collar to apply the choke. In addition, by having his body turned slightly, Royce makes it easy to start any movement to pry Gui's guard open.

Royce's eyes look straight ahead. This helps keep his head straight. If the eyes look down, the head will tip forward, breaking the perfect posture. Keep your eyes looking straight ahead, almost as if you were purposely ignoring what the opponent is doing.

Royce's right hand grabs both Gui's collars at the sternum level. His arm is relaxed and slightly bent to prevent Gui from sitting up. Royce does not need to maintain pressure with a stiff arm, but simply needs to be aware of the possibility of Gui's attempt to sit up. If that happened, Royce would add pressure to Gui's chest to prevent him from raising his chest off the mat. Royce's left hand grabs Gui's belt. His elbow is closed and is inside Gui's right leg to keep Gui from lifting his hips off the ground. Most of the sweeps and armlock attacks begin with the hip high toward the passer's shoulders; by pushing down on Gui's hips, Royce will keep his environment safe from any attacks.

Royce's hips are pushing forward in order to keep perfect posture. The key is to think about pushing your bellybutton forward, forcing your hips forward as well. Many people bend at the hip, which will completely break the posture and make it easy for the opponent to pull you in range of chokes, armlocks, and other attacks. Royce's knees are slightly open outside of Gui's hips for balance. Should his knees be inside the hips, they'd be too close together and Royce would not have balance or the ability to brace to either side. You should have your legs at 90 degrees in relation to each other. Of course that may have to be adjusted for very thin or very large opponents.

By sitting on top of his heels, Royce is ready to spring up or down. If he were to sit on the mat between his feet, he would lose a lot of mobility and become susceptible to being pushed straight back.

Incorrect Posture

Note how Royce's back is curved, head is draped down, and eyes are looking at Gui's chest without any semblance of the perfect alignment discussed above. In this situation, Gui can pull Royce forward almost at will by holding Royce's collar, by pulling his triceps, or by pulling his elbows forward to open them up. Additionally, because Royce's torso is down, Gui can easily grab both collars for a choke. Royce is leaning forward and not sitting on his heels, making it extremely easy for Gui to pull him forward off balance.

Proper Posture Standing

1 Note how Royce's right elbow touches his right thigh, trapping Gui's left leg and hips from moving. Royce's back is straight, with his head in the same line.

2 Once he lifts Gui's hips, Royce's hips are forward and his torso is more perpendicular to the ground. Notice his right elbow is still pressed against his right thigh.

Incorrect Posture Standing

Note how Royce maintained his head down and his hips back, bending at the hips, allowing Gui to lock his legs high over his back. From this position Gui can attack Royce's arms for armlocks or pull him over his head for a reversal.

31. Regaining posture 1

Knowing good posture is not enough. Situations will occur when you have your posture broken by your opponent. Knowing how to regain it is paramount to success.

1 Royce has his posture broken or ends up in bad posture after an exchange.

2 Gui further aggravates the situation by bringing his legs toward his head, driving Royce's body forward and pulling Royce's head down with his right hand.

3 Royce starts by pulling down on Gui's collar, driving his elbows back. At the same time, Royce pushes off his toes, pressing against the mat and leaning even further forward while raising his chest up and away from Gui's chest, creating some space between them.

4 Royce regains his posture by pushing off his right arm and sitting back on his heels. He leans back with his head and drives his hips forward until he has a straight line between his back and head.

32. Regaining posture 2: choke counter

Another situation that occurs frequently when starting to pass the guard is for the opponent to break your posture with his legs, reach over your lead arm with his arm, and drive his elbow down, taking away your ability to stiffen your arm and keep him away.

1 Gui loops his left arm over Royce's right and grabs Royce's left lapel with his hand.

2 Gui breaks Royce's posture by bending his left arm and driving his elbow down on Royce's elbow, preventing him from straightening the arm. Should Royce attempt to stand up or open the guard, he would be susceptible to attacks such as a choke or armlock.

3 Royce counters the posture break and attempted choke by looping his right arm over Gui's left arm again. With his right hand he grabs Gui's left lapel as close to the throat as possible. He steps out with his left leg and pushes his weight forward, driving his right hand with the lapel down on Gui's throat for a choke. Now Royce is ready to either continue the choke, forcing Gui to push Royce away and straighten his legs to relieve the choking pressure, or Royce can simply stand up and break Gui's guard open, or he can go back and regain his posture.

33. Stacking guard pass

This is one of the most traditional guard passes in Gracie jiu-jitsu. It is the first guard pass taught to beginners and remains a very effective way to pass the opponent's guard and reach side-control. In recent years many practitioners shied away from using this type of pass because they ended up caught in a triangle, but if done correctly, with proper posture and mechanics, the passer controls the position the entire time with no danger of submission. The key is to retain proper alignment of your back and head, maintaining perfect posture and foiling the triangle.

1 Royce is in Gui's closed guard. He maintains good posture with a perfect straight line from the bottom of his spine to his head.

2 Royce begins the pass by advancing his right knee and pulling Gui's lapel with his right hand, moving his right elbow until it touches the outside top of his right thigh. Notice that Royce does not slide his hand down but actually pulls the lapel, pulling Gui's torso to Royce's right side. Royce makes sure his elbow touches the outside top of the thigh. If Royce's elbow is in, he would be vulnerable to an armlock from the guard. This will trap Gui's left leg and hip, taking away any space and movement. Note how Royce does not keep the top of his right foot flat on the mat but rather uses his toes, pushing against the mat to keep pressure on Gui.

3 Royce steps out with his left leg, planting the bottom of his foot in line with Gui's hip or slightly back of it. Pushing off that foot, Royce leans further to his right and uses his left leg to support Gui's right leg.

4 Royce slips his left hand inside of Gui's right leg and grabs the outside of the thigh with it. This is a critical point. Royce controls Gui's hips and avoids the triangle by grabbing the right leg with his left arm and by continuing to trap Gui's left leg and hips between his right arm and leg. Notice that Royce's right leg keeps Gui's hips propped up.

5 Royce starts to walk forward with his left foot gaining position on Gui. Notice how Royce maintains his head far away from Gui and keeps the posture at all times. He still controls Gui's right leg with his right arm and the left leg and hips are still trapped by Royce's right arm and leg.

6 Royce continues to walk forward with his left foot, gaining more position on Gui. At this point Royce lets go of the grip on Gui's right leg and props it up to his left shoulder as he grabs his own lapel instead. Many times the defender fights this and has "heavy legs"; in such a case, Royce would dip his torso and shoot the left elbow up to help bring Gui's leg to his shoulder. This allows even more control over Gui's leg. Again, the position of Royce's head is important. You want perfect posture with a straight back and the head almost leaning back, eyes looking forward. Note that Royce's right elbow is out and not in. Should Gui somehow try a triangle, he could not lock his legs around Royce's head or arm and Royce would take advantage of the attack and pass even faster.

7 Royce use his chest to pass as he pushes it against Gui's leg, driving it back. He continues to move forward, taking little steps with his left foot. At this point Royce can either grab his own right wrist (for NHB fights) or Gui's left collar (for jiu-jitsu rules) with his left hand. Royce brings his left knee in, blocking Gui's hips even further. The key here is tightness and posture. Notice how Royce's head is always pointing straight.

8 With his left hand, Royce grabs deep inside Gui's lapel, leading with his thumb in. Royce helps pull himself forward by the left arm, pulling on Gui's collar.

9 In full control of the position and now starting to stack Gui on his head, Royce drops his left knee to the ground next to Gui's right hip and pushes off his right leg, driving forward and stacking Gui. Royce changes his right hand from Gui's right lapel and places it on top of Gui's left biceps. Royce makes sure his elbow is out to avoid an armlock.

9 ***Incorrect 1*** Royce has his right elbow in and Gui easily armlocks him. Keep your elbow out and open to avoid this.

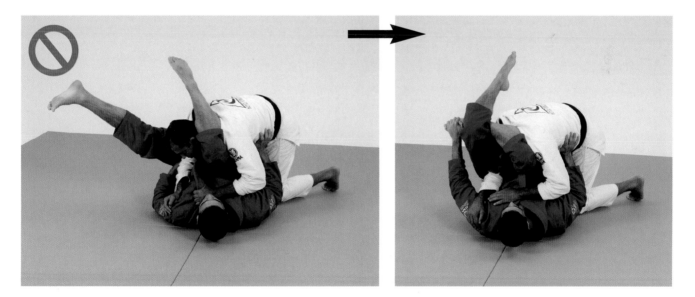

9 ***Incorrect 2*** Royce has his right elbow in and allows his head to drop down and Gui quickly triangles him. You must keep your head up and elbow out to avoid submission when passing this way.

10 Royce continues to walk to his left and stack Gui's body, forcing his legs over his head. He does so by pushing off his legs and feet as he drives his chest up against Gui's thigh. Notice that Royce does not push against Gui's thigh in a line parallel to the mat; that would allow Gui much more leverage and power to resist. Instead, Royce pushes in a diagonal line from his left foot to his head, thus deflecting any power that Gui may have. Notice that Royce maintains pressure with his chest as he moves around Gui's right leg.

11 Royce completes the pass and reaches side-control.

34. Standing guard pass 1

Another forgotten way to pass the guard is the traditional standing guard pass. This is one of Grandmaster Helio Gracie's preferred ways to pass the guard. Royce learned many tricks from his father and uses this one frequently as well. The key to this pass once again is posture, patience, and controlling the opponent at all times.

1 Royce begins to pass Gui's guard. Royce has good posture and feels that everything is safe to begin the pass. Royce grips Gui's lapels near the chest with his hands, pulling them slightly toward himself.

2 Royce swings his torso to his right and props his left leg up, planting the foot right under his body.

3 Royce does a pendulum to his left and props his right foot in a similar position. One of the keys to maintaining balance when swinging the body to prop the leg out is for you to imagine there is a wall in front of your face and you cannot swing forward or back but must stay in the plane of the wall. Keep your head straight during the entire movement. Royce is in a deep squat and controls Gui's hips by keeping his elbows and arms tight against Gui's legs, locking them between his arms and thighs. Royce continues to pull Gui's lapel, bringing his torso in. At this point Gui may struggle, trying to escape his hips or get distance somehow. Royce patiently waits for the proper moment when Gui stops struggling before attempting the next move.

4 Leading with his head and maintaining perfect posture, Royce extends his legs, raising his body and lifting Gui's hips off the mat until he is in base. Notice Royce's legs are slightly bent and his hips are centered in base. Royce retains control of Gui's torso with his right hand on the left lapel. At this point, Gui may open his legs and try to defend the open guard. If that is the case, Royce would skip opening the guard (steps 5 and 6) and go right to step 7.

5 Royce brings his left arm in so that his forearm presses down against Gui's right leg near the knee. Notice that Royce remains in base with his legs slightly flexed and his hips in. Royce will either push down on Gui's right leg until he opens some space to slide his left arm in, or he may reach back and slide the arm in the space near Gui's feet.

6 Royce wraps his left arm around Gui's right thigh and holds it in place. Notice that Royce has not changed his posture and base throughout this movement.

6 *Alternate angle* This angle provides a better view of the action.

7 Royce twists his torso to his right and drives his left arm forward, taking a slight step out with his right foot, forcing Gui's legs open. Notice how Royce's body is now centered over Gui's body. Royce pushes his left knee in toward Gui's right thigh. His hips are tight, pressing against Gui's hips to take away space, and he still has control of the left lapel.

8 Royce opens Gui's lapel with his right hand, creating a guide for his left hand to grab deep in the collar. Royce's hand goes in with the thumb inside. Royce slides the hand down the collar, guiding in the crease between the thumb and index finger until it gets as deep and close to the back of Gui's head as possible. At this point Royce makes sure his right elbow is open so there is no possibility for Gui to armlock him, even if somehow he could move his hips.

9 Royce puts his right hand on Gui's left biceps, keeping the elbow out, and pulls his left arm tight as he drops his weight forward, driving his chest against Gui's right thigh and stacking Gui's legs over his head.

10 Royce slides his chest to his left as he reaches Gui's side. Notice Royce's head posture: As he passes the guard, his head is perpendicular to the ground and his eyes are straight.

11 Royce reaches across-side position.

35. Standing guard pass 2: opponent hooks the leg

Many times when you use a standing pass the defender will hook one of your legs with his arm while keeping the legs closed. In this position he may attempt to execute a sweep by stretching his body and driving his hips forward, forcing you to fall back since you cannot step away and regain base with your right leg trapped. Here is the solution.

1 Royce is executing the standing guard pass, but this time Gui counters by wrapping his left arm inside and around Royce's right leg. At this point Royce needs to worry about his base and posture, otherwise Gui could try a sweep by stretching his body and driving his hips forward, forcing Royce to fall back. Royce counters this by pulling Gui's lapel tight with his right hand while driving his right elbow to his right thigh, shifting his weight to his right side. Once he has reestablished his base, Royce continues as in the previous technique, pushing down on Gui's right leg with the left forearm until it opens.

2 Royce slips his left arm inside the legs and grabs Gui's right thigh while still maintaining his right elbow on his right thigh and his weight on his right side.

3 Pushing off his left foot, Royce turns his body to his right, driving his hips forward. Royce turns his torso to his right, turning Gui's leg with it and stacking him. Notice Royce's back and head posture and the straight line from his tailbone to the top of his head for perfect posture.

4 Royce slides his left hand deep in Gui's collar and pulls it tight as he drives his chest forward, forcing Gui's right thigh down over his own head.

5 Royce continues to drive his chest forward, turning Gui over his head. He twists his torso to the right to reach Gui's right side. At this point Gui may attempt to roll over his left shoulder and reach all fours to defend the guard pass. Royce uses the right hand on Gui's hip or pant leg to prevent him from rolling over.

6 Royce completes the guard pass and reaches side-control on Gui.

36. NHB guard pass 1

Opening the legs and avoiding a submission or a sweep is difficult enough in sports jiu-jitsu; once you introduce the element of strikes, it becomes daunting. Royce takes advantage of this fact and uses strikes to create chaos and force his opponent to open his legs to defend the blows, allowing Royce to reach the side. While many jiu-jitsu guard passes are effective in street fights or NHB situations, this one offers many advantages over the rest.

1 Royce is in a typical guard stance for a street fight. He blocks Gui's arms from striking him by placing his hands on top of Gui's biceps and keeping the elbows down. From this position, Royce can follow Gui's arms even if Gui tries to circle them under the hands to try to evade the block and strike.

2 Pushing off both feet, Royce leans forward, head-butting Gui in the chin. If head-butts are not allowed by event rules, Royce would lean forward and drive his head against the side of Gui's head to cause discomfort.

3 Royce pushes off his hands and quickly jumps up. Notice Royce's feet position, each slightly wider than Gui's hips for base. His knees are in and his hips are pushing forward against Gui's legs, forcing them back.

4 Royce delivers a series of blows to Gui's face as he continues to push his hips and weight forward on Gui's legs. Gui tries to extend his hips and legs to create distance and take away the power of Royce's punches. Royce extends his body so his chest is behind Gui's legs.

5 With his left hand, Royce grabs the back of Gui's right ankle . . .

6 And pushes it down, stacking Gui's legs over his head.

7 Royce changes hands and grabs Gui's ankle with his right hand.

8 Royce steps out to his left with his left leg, brings his right leg around Gui's body, and uses his right knee to push Gui's hips to the side, reaching his side.

9 Royce puts his right knee on Gui's stomach for the guard pass and is in position to continue striking Gui.

37. NHB guard pass 2: footlock

In the fast-paced and violent world of street fighting and NHB, the mayhem created by strikes can lead to many submission opportunities. In this case, Royce takes advantage of the attacks and goes for a footlock. This option is actually available from many of the standing guard passes in jiu-jitsu, even in sports situations.

1 Royce is delivering a series of blows to Gui's head and Gui has opened the legs to defend himself.

2 As Gui extends the legs to drive Royce away from striking distance, Royce brings his right elbow to his right thigh, trapping Gui's left leg. Royce closes the figure-four around Gui's ankle by looping his right arm around Gui's left ankle, locking the hand on his own left wrist while his left hand grabs Gui's left ankle. Royce slides his left knee between Gui's legs so that his knee pushes on the crotch.

3 Royce leans back to his right as he drives his left knee toward the mat.

4 Royce leans back, applying the footlock. He bends Gui's foot back with the armpit pushing the toes and applies pressure to the Achilles' heel with the blade of his right forearm, pushing up on it while he drives his left knee forward between Gui's legs.

5 For even more pressure, Royce will crank the lock by arching back for a painful foot-and-knee lock.

6 Alternatively, from step 3, Royce can simply fall back to the mat and extend the foot as he grabs Gui's right ankle with the left hand and uses his left foot to push the thigh, keeping Gui from sitting up and coming over the top to defend the position.

38. Spider guard pass 1

Dealing with the spider guard presents its own set of problems. The spider guard is typically a sports guard. Since it involves holding both sleeves and pressing one or both feet against the passer's biceps to control his movement, the defender can make it very difficult for the passer to release control on the sleeves and find the grip and control necessary to effectively pass. In most cases, Royce uses his hips and knees to deflect the power of the legs, rather than fight to release the grip on the sleeve.

1 Royce is in Gui's spider guard. In this case, Gui has his right foot pushing against Royce's left biceps and left foot pushing the hips.

2 Instead of fighting to release Gui's grip on his sleeves, Royce grabs Gui's pants with his hands and makes clever use of his legs. He walks forward, drives his right knee against Gui's left thigh, and pushes down on it, effectively taking away any pressure against his hips. The same exact move should be used in cases where both feet are against the biceps.

3 Having released the block of Gui's left foot against his hips, Royce pushes his hips forward, forcing Gui's legs back. Notice how Royce uses his hips against Gui's right leg to push the leg over on top of Gui's head, stacking him.

4 Royce continues to drive his weight forward on top of Gui's right leg, further stacking him. Royce then grabs Gui's left lapel with his left hand, thumb in, and helps pull himself down with it. Notice how Royce has extreme pressure on Gui, stacking his legs over his body. Royce's hips push down on Gui's right leg while his right knee presses down on the left leg.

5 Royce passes the guard by twisting his body toward his right, flinging Gui's right leg out of the way.

6 Royce adjusts the side-control position with his left elbow tight against Gui's left ear, his right hand planted on the mat next to Gui's right hip, and his chest pressing down against Gui's chest.

39. Spider guard pass 2: inside option

At times when you use the previous technique to pass the guard, the smart defender will bend his leg down, effectively blocking the pass around the high leg. In that case, you simply change your approach and pass through the inside of the legs by dropping your knee in. Once again, notice that many of the pass movements and actions are interchangeable. The principles of applying pressure and deflecting power and using your hips and chest to pass are present in most if not all of these techniques, so master the concepts, experiment with the alternatives, and be ready to use the principles in other situations you may face that are not demonstrated here. Notice that Royce simply reacts to any blocks and obstacle that appear in front of him, much like water finds its way around any rock in the riverbed. If the rock or the obstacle moves, Royce simply flows around it rather than fight against it!

1 Royce has reached the same position as in technique 38, step 2. His right knee pushing down on Gui's left leg has released the block against his hips and Royce is proceeding with the guard pass, walking forward and pushing his hips against Gui's right leg to stack him.

2 Gui smartly bends and drops his right leg, blocking Royce's path to Gui's right to reach side-control. Notice that this move effectively stops Royce from throwing his hips forward to fling Gui's right leg out of the way.

3 When faced with one door closed, Royce looks for another to open. He twists his body to his left (counterclockwise) and drives his right knee all the way to the mat while still maintaining his right foot hooked over Gui's leg to keep him from locking the legs and trapping Royce in a half-guard.

4 Royce continues to pass through the inside. He drops his chest to Gui's chest, using his right arm to hug the head for control. Notice that Royce has not yet released the right foot hook on Gui's left leg.

5 Royce maintains his hook on Gui's left leg and uses his left arm to hook Gui's right leg as he loops his left leg over. Although this position appears unstable for Royce, it is not, so long as he does the following: It is very important for Royce to maintain his right shoulder pressed against the left side of Gui's face with his arm wrapped around the head to keep Gui from turning to his own left and facing Royce. In addition, Royce needs to keep Gui's right leg from dropping and reaching the ground, where he could push off it and roll over the top of Royce.

6 Royce lands the left leg on the mat with his hips facing up and his control over Gui's head and right leg still in place. At this point, Royce can release the right foot hook over the left leg.

7 Royce switches his hips back so they face the mat by sliding the right leg under his body until he achieves perfect side-control position.

PASSING THE HALF-GUARD

It is extremely common to end up in the half-guard when passing someone's guard. In fact, today many sports fighters have developed a variety of attacks and sweeps from the half-guard and actually jump to it any chance they get without even attempting to go for the full guard. Regardless of the way you end up in the half-guard, being able to effectively pass and attack from the half-guard is a must in Gracie jiu-jitsu. The keys are to try to keep the opponent's back flat on the mat, to free up the trapped knee from between the legs, to maintain your balance and control over the opponent, and especially not to be in a hurry to pass, but rather take your time and make certain that your moves are stable and secure.

40. Half-guard pass 1: choke

Opportunities occur for attacks in many situations in Gracie jiu-jitsu, and it is no different for the half-guard. Actually, as the defender feels he is in control or is going for a sweep, many times he is not aware of the dangers around him, so the half-guard offers a variety of openings for submissions, especially chokes. In this technique, Royce immediately takes advantage of an opening and goes for a choke from the half-guard.

1 Royce is in Gui's half-guard. Gui has turned toward Royce, his left arm inside Royce's left leg while the right one grabs the belt around Royce's right ribs and his legs trap Royce's right leg. From this point, Gui can execute a few sweeps. Royce's first objective is to keep Gui from getting under him, so Royce keeps pressure with his left leg as he tries to extend it. Should Gui be successful getting inside and under Royce, a sweep will be almost inevitable.

2 Royce sees the opportunity for a choke, so he gives up some space between his chest and Gui's chest by arching his back. He wraps his left arm around Gui's neck until his hand grabs his own right lapel. This is only possible because Gui is turned toward Royce. Should Gui decide that Royce's attack is too dangerous, he would retreat and put his back on the mat, which would nullify the sweep threat for Royce. In this case, however, Gui persists.

3 *Detail* Notice how Royce's hand grabs his own right lapel, reaching with the palm facing out toward his own chest.

3 Royce reaches deep with his left hand, grabbing his own collar.

4 Once in control of the lapel, Royce cinches the grip and sprawls, stretching his leg and pushing his hips in. This will tighten the lapel choke around Gui's neck.

41. Half-guard pass 2: mount

While many people prefer to follow the normal hierarchy of positions and pass to side-control, the half-guard allows you to bypass that and go directly to the mount. Royce prefers to take whatever the opponent gives him, but he also prefers to go to the best position available. If the mount is available he will take that over side-control.

1 Royce is in Gui's half-guard with his right leg trapped between Gui's legs. Gui has turned on his right side. Royce's first concern is to keep Gui from reversing him, so he controls the position by grabbing Gui's belt with his left hand and locking his elbow tight against Gui's neck.

2 Royce coils his right arm back and braces his forearm against Gui's left thigh. Pushing off it, Royce slides his hips back, creating space for the right leg to slide out. Royce continues bracing and pushing Gui's thigh down until his right knee clears the grasp of Gui's legs. Notice that at the same time Royce is pushing his body up toward Gui's head and using his left arm to push the head to the right for a neck crank. The pressure will force Gui to release the half-guard.

2 *Reverse Angle* Notice Royce's elbow pushing against Gui's left thigh as close to the knee as possible.

3 Royce continues to drive his knee out until his foot escapes. He drives his right knee toward the mat as he rolls over, putting Gui's back on the ground.

4 Having reached the mount, Royce releases the grip on Gui's belt and places his arms and legs in proper position for base.

42. half-guard pass 3: side-control with armlock

At times when in the half-guard, your opponent has turned so much and curls himself so tight that it may be hard to execute the guard pass to the mount. In that case, Royce uses the same approach as before to release his knee, but turns it inside and goes for the across-side position instead.

1 Royce is in Gui's half-guard with his right leg trapped between Gui's legs. He starts out by placing his right forearm against Gui's right thigh, bracing it with the elbow as close to the knee as possible. Notice how Gui has turned to his own right side. Royce controls the position by holding Gui's belt with his left arm and pulling it tight, driving his elbow against Gui's head.

2 Since Gui is turned on his side too much and has coiled his body so tight, Royce decides it is better to go to side-control. He opens his right leg, planting the foot on the mat. Pushing off the leg, Royce raises his hips while still pushing Gui's left thigh away with his right elbow. Notice that by raising the hips Royce creates a lot of space between himself and Gui. Royce continues to push and slide his leg until his right knee clears the grip of Gui's legs.

3 Once the knee has cleared, Royce plants his right hand on the mat, twists his hips to his own left, turns the knee to the inside, and aims it toward the mat on Gui's right side as he opens his left leg wide for base.

4 Still bracing off his right arm and left leg, Royce continues to drive his right knee in and up toward Gui's head. He does that by pushing his hips forward toward Gui's head. At the same time, Royce uses his left hand to control Gui's right arm, grabbing under the right elbow and forcing Gui to turn so that his back is flat on the mat.

5 Royce continues to drive his hips forward as he pulls on Gui's right arm until his right foot releases from between Gui's legs. Royce is now in side-control with his hips facing Gui's head.

6 *Alternate Angle* From this angle, we can see that Royce may opt to apply an arm bar as he leans back and loops his left leg over Gui's head.

7 Once his foot lands next to Gui's left ear, Royce applies pressure to the elbow by arching his back, driving Gui's right wrist down with his armpit and forcing his hips forward against the elbow for the submission.

43. Half-guard pass 4: cross-choke

The cross-choke is one of the best options for a submission from the half-guard. As the opponent struggles to achieve the proper position for a sweep, many times engaging both legs and one arm to achieve the proper position, he leaves his neck open for a choke, often with only one arm to defend. To your and his surprise, many times he is so engaged in accomplishing the sweep that he does not even realize the attack is coming.

1 Royce is in Gui's half-guard with his right leg trapped between Gui's legs. Gui is setting up a sweep and wraps his right arm inside Royce's left leg. Should Royce allow Gui to turn in and get himself under Royce's body, he would be very vulnerable for a sweep. So the first order of business for Royce is to keep his left leg back and keep Gui's body away from his.

2 Royce lifts his torso and wraps his right arm around Gui's left arm. Royce uses his left hand to open Gui's right collar and gives it to his own right hand. Royce may aid the control of this position by putting his weight back on his left leg, locking Gui's right arm with his left leg.

3 Royce grabs Gui's left collar with his left hand. In this case he leads with the thumb in and grabs very deep, but if that is too difficult he can just grab the gi on the outside of the left shoulder.

4 Royce applies the choke by bringing his elbows together and pulling the collar toward his chest. He adds pressure by driving his left elbow down toward the mat, forcing it against Gui's throat.

44. Half-guard pass 5: opponent escapes cross-choke

A common occurrence during the previous attack is for the smart opponent, sensing the cross-choke coming, to create some space, release the half-guard, push himself away, and get to his knees. In that case, you apply a takedown to get to side-control. We pick up the position from step 43.2.

1 Royce has wrapped his right arm around Gui's left arm and has his right hand grabbing Gui's right collar. Sensing the choke coming, Gui removes his right arm from inside Royce's left leg and uses it to push the left knee. Gui releases the half-guard as he escapes his hips away from Royce.

2 Gui escapes his hips and turns to his knees. From this point, Gui can try to come forward and force Royce back to the mat for a reversal or he may pull guard or attempt a sweep.

3 Royce maintains his right arm wrapped around Gui's left arm and the handgrip on the collar. He uses his left hand or left knee to pull Gui's right arm off the ground, taking away Gui's base.

4 Royce spins his torso to his own left and continues to pull Gui's right arm in as he throws his own right shoulder forward, pulling Gui's collar up with the right hand and twisting Gui counterclockwise.

5 Royce continues the movement until he has spun Gui, landing in side-control.

45. Half-guard pass 6: Kimura

One of Royce's favorite attacks from the half-guard is the Kimura. Generally in the half-guard the defender has his arm wrapped under the attacker's armpit and his legs are trapping the leg, allowing the Kimura attack to be executed. Look for it and you will see the opening in many half-guard situations. The beauty of this attack is that it forces the defender to either submit or quickly release the half-guard to avoid the submission.

1 Royce is in Gui's half-guard with his right leg trapped. Gui's left arm is under Royce's right armpit in normal half-guard posture.

2 While maintaining his left elbow on the ground pushing against Gui's head, Royce leans back, reaching with his right hand until it grabs Gui's left wrist.

3 Royce moves his torso back over Gui's chest, driving the left arm to the ground. Royce locks the figure-four around Gui's left arm with his own left arm wrapped under Gui's, locking the hand onto his right wrist.

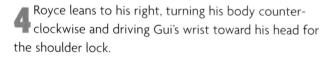

4 Royce leans to his right, turning his body counter-clockwise and driving Gui's wrist toward his head for the shoulder lock.

SIDE-CONTROL

Side-control is a very important yet misunderstood and neglected position. Most people think of it as a place to rest after you pass the guard, but that is not so. Side-control is a very good position from which to attack if you know what to do. It is not necessary to leave this very stable position and go for a less stable knee-on-stomach or mount to attack. On the other hand, side-control opens an array of finishing techniques. It is an excellent transitory position to the back and mounts.

The key to attacking from side-control is to have the attack options ready and be able to quickly switch between them, instead of fighting against the opponent's escape. If you apply a lot of pressure to your opponent he will give you an arm, a neck, or something. The other key is to control the head, especially when the hips are facing forward. If you don't control the head you allow the opponent to escape to your back, but if you maintain control of the head that will not happen. Another common mistake is that you control the head and work tight, but you release the pressure when you attack. You need to keep the pressure at all times. Controlling the opponent at all times will give you the opportunities you need to finish him.

46. Side-control to mount 1: knee slide

In Gracie jiu-jitsu positional hierarchy, being in the mount or on the back is better than being in side-control, therefore advancing in the positional ladder (see page 296) should be one of the objectives of a fighter. From side-control, reaching the mount is one of the most natural advancements you can make. Royce loves being in the mount in total control of the opponent, so he will demonstrate a variety of ways to reach the mount from side-control. In this case, Royce simply slides his knee over the opponent's stomach until the leg reaches the other side and he ends up mounted. This technique works best against beginners, although it can work against advanced practitioners if you have the element of surprise or can trap the arm, as shown in the next technique.

1 Royce has reached side-control on Pedro. He has his left elbow pressing against the left side of Pedro's head, keeping him from turning and creating space to escape. Royce's right hand is planted on the mat next to Pedro's right hip, preventing him from bringing his right knee in and replacing the guard. Royce's chest presses against Pedro's chest, pinning him to the mat.

2 With this type of side-control, Royce's left arm is blocking Pedro from seeing what is happening below, so he begins the technique by sliding his right knee just inside his own right arm over Pedro's stomach.

3 Royce continues to slide the right knee over Pedro's stomach and uses his right hand to push Pedro's left leg in, preventing Pedro from opening it out, which would make it more difficult for Royce's leg to reach the other side. Notice that Royce's right foot is hooked on Pedro's right thigh.

4 Royce drives his right knee down toward the mat as he releases his right foot from Pedro's thigh and loops it over the knees.

5 Royce's right leg touches the ground next to Pedro's left side, completing the mount.

47. Side-control to mount 2: knee-slide variation—clearing the arm

Many times a fighter will defend the knee slide by keeping his arm framed against the attacker's hip, blocking the attacker's ability to bring the hip over for the mount. When faced with that situation, Royce simply uses his hips to clear the arm and lock it in place.

1 Royce is across-side on Pedro with his left elbow tight against the left side of Pedro's head and his right hand blocking Pedro's right hip. Pedro maintains good posture and keeps his right forearm blocking Royce's hips, preventing him from getting close and attempting to mount.

2 Royce knows he has to clear Pedro's right arm, so he turns his hips in by planting his right foot on the mat and sliding his left leg toward Pedro's feet until his hips have deflected Pedro's arm and cleared the right elbow. At this point, Royce's left hip is touching the ground and is in front of Pedro's right elbow.

3 Once he has his left hip in front of Pedro's right elbow, Royce simply brings his hips square with Pedro by bringing the left leg back so that his left knee touches near Pedro's head. Royce makes sure when bringing the leg back that his knee slides close to Pedro's right side so that his left hip and leg will drive Pedro's right arm back. Notice how Pedro's right arm ends up locked between Royce's left leg and his own head.

4 Royce drives the left knee forward until it touches Pedro's head, taking away any gaps that may allow Pedro to remove the arm and bring it back for a block once again. At the same time, Royce uses his right arm to pull up on Pedro's left arm, keeping him from using it to block Royce's right knee from sliding over. At this point, Royce is in total control of Pedro and can start to mount.

5 Royce slides the tip of his right knee over Pedro's stomach and drives it toward the left side of Pedro's hips.

6 Once Royce's right knee touches Pedro's left elbow, Royce can release the grip on that arm and simply continue to slide the knee over the stomach. Notice Royce's right foot hooked on Pedro's right hip to prevent Pedro from trapping it for a half-guard.

7 Royce drives his right knee to the mat and loops his foot over Pedro's legs until he ends up mounted.

48. Side-control to mount 3: knee slide—opponent blocks knee

Many times when you attempt the knee-slide method, the opponent will use his outside arm to block the knee slide. Royce shows a clever way to deal with the situation and actually achieve even greater control over the opponent. We begin the position with Royce's knee already sliding over Pedro's stomach after Royce has cleared the near arm. The technique, however, works whether the arm is cleared or not.

1 Royce is sliding his right knee over Pedro's stomach in an attempt to reach the mount. Pedro uses his outside arm to block the knee slide as he pushes with his left hand against Royce's knee. Royce could try to muscle through the block but, depending on the opponent's strength, it may be difficult. Royce prefers to use his intelligence and simply deflect the power and use it to his advantage.

2 Royce slides his right hand between Pedro's left arm and body, right in the gap near the elbow. Royce plants the palm of the hand on the mat.

3 Royce walks his right hand up as he drives Pedro's left arm off the mat and toward his head. Notice that at this point Royce has great control over Pedro's upper body: Pedro's right arm is trapped between Royce's left leg and body and left arm is controlled by Royce's right arm.

4 Royce continues to walk his right hand up, creating enough space to continue with the knee slide until his right knee touches the ground and he is mounted.

5 Royce adjust his mount while still keeping his right arm under Pedro's left arm.

49. Side-control to mount 4: leg-over method

Another simple and yet very effective way to achieve the mount is the leg-over method. In this method, Royce simply switches the hips and loops his leg over the opponent's legs for the mount. It is quite a simple method, but it works surprisingly well either alone or in connection with another attack. There are two keys for success. One is for Royce to make sure he blocks Pedro's vision of what is happening below. The second is for Royce to keep his body as still as possible as he loops the leg over, catching Pedro by surprise. By practicing the move repeatedly and concentrating on the lightness of the action, you will be surprised at how still you can keep your upper body while looping the leg over.

1 Royce has side-control on Pedro with his left elbow tight against the right side of Pedro's head to keep Pedro from moving, and his right hand next to Pedro's right hip to prevent Pedro from bringing his right knee in and replacing the guard.

2 *Alternate Angle* Royce switches the hips by planting his right foot on the mat and driving his left leg forward until his left thigh and knee are touching Pedro's right side. Royce places his right hand on Pedro's left hip. Notice that Royce's hips now aim toward Pedro's feet. At this point, Royce would pause the action and might take a deep breath, appearing to stop and evaluate the situation.

3 While keeping his upper body as still as possible, Royce loops his right leg over Pedro's legs. To keep the movement to a minimum, Royce braces off his left elbow and left leg, ensuring that his body doesn't flinch as he loops the leg over. This is very important; otherwise Pedro will sense something happening and react by either lifting his legs or turning to the side and starting to escape his hips. Royce may help the move with his right hand pushing Pedro's left leg over to the right, making a shorter way for his leg to loop over. Notice that Royce will only push the knee at the last moment; otherwise he alerts Pedro that something is happening. Also note that although Pedro has both his feet on the ground, as a beginner would, the move works equally well if Pedro has his right foot on top of the left knee with the right knee high to try to block the mount.

4 Royce plants his right foot on the mat next to Pedro's left hip. Up to this point the entire move should occur almost imperceptibly, but once the foot hits the mat, Pedro will know that he is being mounted and will try to escape his hips to his left and bring his right knee under Royce's left leg to initiate the escape. Therefore, it is imperative that Royce maintain his left hip on the mat.

5 Royce brings his left knee up between Pedro's body and right arm, completing the mount.

6 Royce brings his left elbow to the right side of Pedro's head, planting his hands on each side of the head for complete balance and control of the mount.

50. Side-control to mount 5: leg-over method—opponent has both arms in

Sometimes when you are in side-control, your opponent will have his arms in against his chest rather than the standard position of one under the armpit and one under the body. In such a situation, the leg-over method has to be adjusted; otherwise the opponent will extend his arms and push you off as you loop the leg over. Royce demonstrates a useful variation here.

1 Royce has side-control on Pedro. His left elbow is tight against the right side of the head to keep Pedro from moving, and his right hand is next to Pedro's right hip to prevent him from bringing his right knee in and replacing the guard. Notice that in this case Pedro has his elbows tight against his body and his forearms pressing against his chest. Should Royce try the leg-over method without the adjustment, Pedro would simply push him off.

2 Royce switches the hips by planting his right foot on the mat and driving his left leg forward. Notice that Royce's hips now aim toward Pedro's feet, his left thigh is next to Pedro's right ribcage, and his left knee touches Pedro's right hip. Because Pedro's arms are coiled, instead of having his right hand on Pedro's right hip in preparation for the mount, Royce slides his right arm under Pedro's elbows and grabs Pedro's left elbow with his right hand. At this point, Royce would pause the action and might take a deep breath, appearing to stop and evaluate the situation.

3 While maintaining his upper body as still as possible, Royce loops his right leg over Pedro's legs. To keep the movement to a minimum, Royce braces off his left elbow and left leg, ensuring that his body doesn't flinch as he loops the leg over.

4 Royce plants his right foot on the mat next to Pedro's left hip. Up to this point the entire move should occur almost imperceptibly. This time, since he is holding Pedro's arms tight and pushing them up, Royce has more control over Pedro than in the previous leg-over method and does not have to worry about Pedro escaping his hips to his left, so Royce does not have to keep his left leg on the mat. Instead, he pushes off his right foot and drives his body up on Pedro, forcing Pedro's arms up even more and creating more space for Royce to mount.

5 Royce brings his left knee up between Pedro's body and right arm, completing the mount.

6 Royce brings his left elbow to the right side of Pedro's head, planting his hands on each side of the head for complete balance and control of the mount.

51. Side-control to mount 6: knee-slide variation—locking the belt

A very good option for the knee slide is locking the belt. You hold the opponent's belt by wrapping your arm under and around his shoulder until you can grab the belt. Once you have that lock, you have extreme control over the opponent's upper body and can calmly proceed with the knee slide. This move is most effective when your opponent's opposite arm is under your chest and not under your armpit; otherwise he can slide the arm out as he bridges up.

1 Royce has reached side-control on Pedro. He has his left elbow pressing against the left side of Pedro's head, keeping him from turning and creating space to escape. Royce's right hand is planted on the mat next to Pedro's right hip, preventing him from bringing his right knee in and replacing the guard. Royce's chest presses against Pedro's chest, pinning him to the mat. Pedro has his right arm in, pushing against Royce's chest.

2 Royce senses that Pedro's outside arm is pressing against his chest and opts to use the locking-the-belt method. He wraps his left arm under Pedro's left shoulder and reaches until he grabs Pedro's belt with his left hand.

2 *Detail* Note how Royce grabs Pedro's belt, reaching with the palm of his hand under the belt and locking his fingers as he pulls the belt up toward his shoulder, making a very tight grip around Pedro's left arm and shoulder and locking Pedro's left arm in.

3 Royce slides his right knee over Pedro's stomach.

4 Royce drives his right knee down toward the mat, using his right hand to push Pedro's left knee in.

5 Royce's right leg touches the ground next to Pedro's left side, completing the mount.

52. Side-control to mount 7: leg-over method—locking the belt

A similar variation to the leg-over method involves the opponent having his outside arm in. In that case, Royce may opt to grab the opponent's belt after wrapping his arm around the shoulder. This is similar to the knee-slide lock-the-belt method but with the leg over. Many of these moves and techniques can be interchanged. The locking-the-belt option can be used when both arms are in and you want to use the leg-over technique shown in technique 50.

1 Royce is across-side on Pedro and Pedro has his outside arm in against his own chest. Royce wraps his left arm around Pedro's left shoulder and grabs Pedro's belt with his hand, pulling the belt up tight toward his head.

2 Royce loops his right leg over Pedro's legs while maintaining tight control over Pedro's upper body.

3 Royce slams his right foot on the mat next to Pedro's left thigh and plants his right hand on the mat just under Pedro's left elbow.

4 Notice where Royce's right foot landed next to Pedro's thigh. From there, all he has to do is drop his right knee down to the mat for the mount as he walks his right hand up, forcing Pedro's left elbow up with it.

5 Royce completes the mount by placing his hands on the sides of Pedro's head for balance.

6 *Variation:* If both Pedro's arms are in, Royce adjusts by grabbing under Pedro's arms with his right arm while his left hand locks the belt.

7 Royce loops the leg over for the mount . . .

8 Until his foot touches the mat near Pedro's thigh.

53. Side-control to mount 8: leg-over method—pulling the foot

When you are across-side your opponent is aware that one of your objectives is to reach the mount, so he often closes himself up by placing his inside foot on top of his other knee. His inside leg closes some of the gap on his torso, blocking the mount. Most of the previous methods work even in that case, but with some adjustments, such as having greater flexibility or by pulling or pushing the knee over. Royce, however, prefers the pull-the-foot and mount method. Again, the key to this move is to be subtle when guiding the foot over. The less movement you allow your upper body, the more effective this technique will be.

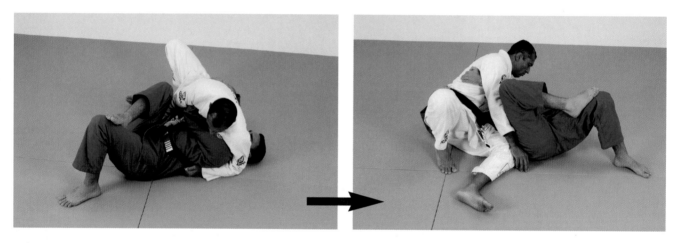

1 These two views show Royce across-side on Pedro with his hips switched, facing Pedro's feet. Pedro has his right foot on top of his left knee so that his right knee and thigh take away much of the gap where Royce would normally either slide his knee or loop his leg for the mount. Royce has his left arm wrapped around Pedro's left shoulder and hand grabbing Pedro's belt. Notice Pedro's arms posture: The right arm is under Royce and the left arm is under Royce's right armpit.

2 With his right hand, Royce grabs the tip of his right foot, pulling it toward his own head as much as his flexibility will allow as he leans back slightly.

3 Using his right hand, Royce quietly guides the right foot through the gap between Pedro's knee and Royce's own torso. By using the hand to pull and guide the foot, Royce can direct the foot through places that he wouldn't normally be able to.

4 Royce continues to guide the foot over Pedro's stomach until it is clear on the opposite side of the hips, locking the heel on Pedro's left thigh. At this point he lets go of the foot.

4 *Reverse angle* Notice how Royce guides his foot until the heel touches Pedro's left thigh. This is very important for tightness and control. It allows Royce to drive his heel against Pedro's thigh as he extends the left leg, sliding the heel on the mat as he mounts.

5 Royce completes the mount by driving off his right foot and pushing his right knee up toward Pedro's head.

54. Side-control to mount 9: opponent has leg up

Another common and effective way to block the mount is for the defender to have his near leg up to close the gap over his stomach, blocking any attempts to drive the knee through or loop the leg over. When having the leg up to block the mount, the defender usually has his foot up high and leg semi-extended, and he will move it up and down slightly, reacting to any attempts to mount. In that situation, Royce once again takes advantage of what the opponent gives to him and uses his right leg to lock the opponent's legs for the mount.

1 Royce is across-side on Pedro with his hips facing down. He has his left arm wrapped around Pedro's left arm with his hand locked on Pedro's belt. Pedro raises his right leg to block Royce's attempt at mounting via the knee slide or leg-over. Royce initiates the technique by using his right arm under Pedro's right knee to keep him from bringing the leg down.

2 Of course Royce cannot wait too long before making his next move, because Pedro's leg is more powerful than Royce's arm, so he quickly loops his right leg over Pedro's left knee and under the right leg (in between Pedro's legs) until his right heel touches the middle of Pedro's left thigh. This detail is very important; Royce will leverage off his heel to twist Pedro's legs. As Royce extends his right leg he presses his heel against Pedro's left thigh, forcing it to the right until he plants the right foot on the mat.

3 Royce pushes off his right foot and drives his knee forward, forcing Pedro's right leg down. At this point Pedro is all twisted up.

4 Royce leans back slightly to create some space between his chest and Pedro's body and slips his right hand inside Pedro's left arm.

5 Royce walks his right hand on the mat, driving Pedro's left arm up and keeping it from blocking the knee.

6 Royce drops his right knee down toward the mat while making sure he has his toes on the mat and the bottom of his right foot pressing against Pedro's left leg.

7 Once his right knee touches the mat, Royce loops his foot over Pedro's right leg and hooks it under for the mount.

55. Side-control to mount 10: trapping the arm

Another Royce favorite to reach the mount from side-control is to trap the inside arm. Royce cleverly uses movement and cunning to trap Pedro's arm, locking it out of use before he slides the knee over for the mount. Notice that in this case Pedro's arms are in close to his chest, but the technique works even if the outside arm is under the armpit. The important thing is to have the near arm curled in either in front of the chest or with the forearm blocking Royce's hips.

1 Royce is across-side on Pedro. Pedro has both arms tight against his chest. Royce has his left elbow tight against Pedro's left ear to keep his head from turning and his right hand on the mat next to Pedro's right hip to prevent him from bringing his left leg in and replacing the guard.

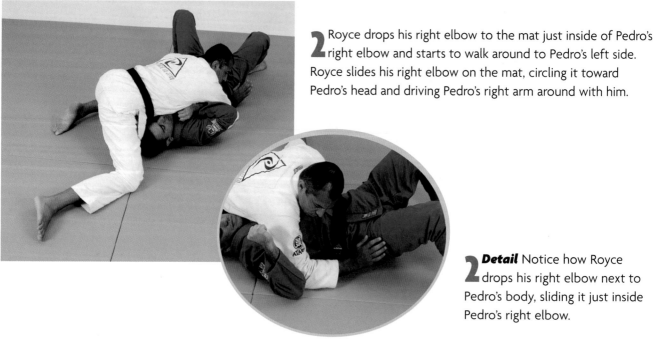

2 Royce drops his right elbow to the mat just inside of Pedro's right elbow and starts to walk around to Pedro's left side. Royce slides his right elbow on the mat, circling it toward Pedro's head and driving Pedro's right arm around with him.

2 *Detail* Notice how Royce drops his right elbow next to Pedro's body, sliding it just inside Pedro's right elbow.

3 Royce continues to walk around to Pedro's left side while bringing his right arm around. Pedro's right arm is not strong enough to prevent Royce from moving to his left and it ends up trapped between Royce's arm and body near the armpit.

4 Once he reaches Pedro's left side, Royce wraps his right arm under Pedro's head, completely locking Pedro's right arm as he drives his chest down against Pedro's chest. Pedro is in a very uncomfortable position here, his arm trapped under Royce. With his left hand, Royce grabs Pedro's left sleeve.

5 Having cleared the arm, there are no obstacles stopping Royce from mounting by sliding his left knee over Pedro's stomach as he brings Pedro's left arm over with him.

6 Royce ends up mounted on Pedro with Pedro's arms crossed under him.

56. Side-control transition attack 1: choke

While executing certain techniques, various opportunities for submissions occur, especially when you are going for the mount. In the previous technique shown, there is an opportunity for a choke that exists just about every time you apply the move. Royce here demonstrates that choke. Fighters have to choose whether to achieve the next position or go for a submission. We pick up the move from the point where Royce has trapped Pedro's elbow and is moving to his left.

1 Royce is moving from side-control to Pedro's left and has trapped Pedro's right arm with his right arm as he drives his right elbow around the mat.

2 As he starts to reach Pedro's left side, Royce slips his left hand inside Pedro's left arm at the elbow. Notice how Royce has his weight on the right elbow and chest, keeping Pedro pinned under him.

3 Royce continues with his left arm until it reaches the collar behind Pedro's head. Once he grips the collar, Royce releases his right elbow from the mat and reaches with the right hand for Pedro's right lapel.

4 Royce grips the inside of Pedro's right lapel, thumb in and fingers on the outside, and drives his right elbow to the ground on top of Pedro's throat for the choke.

4 **Detail** Note how Royce grips Pedro's lapel with his right hand: the thumb is in and the fingers are out so that the blade of his forearm is against Pedro's throat. When Royce drops the elbow to the mat, he will choke Pedro. If necessary, Royce can circle the right elbow toward Pedro's right shoulder to apply additional choking pressure.

57. Side-control transition attack 2: armlock

Another submission available when transitioning from side to side in side-control, especially when using the elbow slide to trap the arm (technique 55) is the armlock. In this case, rather than going for the choke, Royce chooses to go for the armlock. He may do so because Pedro keeps his left arm tight against his chest (making it difficult for Royce to slip his left hand in, as in the previous technique) or simply because he feels more comfortable with the armlock than with the choke. Again, we pick up the technique as Royce transitions from one side to the other after trapping Pedro's arm with his elbow on the mat.

1 Royce is transitioning from Pedro's left side to his right after having trapped the right arm with his right elbow. Royce starts the armlock attack by driving his left hand under Pedro's left arm.

2 Royce grabs Pedro's left wrist with his right hand and wraps his left arm under Pedro's left arm until he locks his hand on his own right wrist for total arm control.

3 Royce raises his torso so that he can step over Pedro's head with his right leg. Notice that Royce plants his right foot right next to Pedro's head, taking away any space for an escape.

4 Royce puts his left knee on Pedro's stomach while still controlling Pedro's left arm. Notice how Royce's hips are low and tight against Pedro's left arm to keep him from pulling his left elbow down and escaping the armlock.

5 Royce brings both knees together, further locking Pedro's arm as he leans back, and drops his back to the mat, pulling Pedro's left arm with him.

6 Royce completes the armlock with his back on the mat as he drives his hips up against Pedro's left elbow and keeps Pedro's wrist tight against his chest, hyperextending the elbow joint.

58. Side-control transition attack 3: Kimura

Another submission option available when transitioning from side to side in side-control, especially when using the elbow slide to trap the arm (technique 55), is the Kimura. The setup for the technique is similar to the one in technique 57, so you now have three different options for submissions from one transition. These options may occur in various other transitions when the arms are in different positions than the ones shown; the important thing to remember is that these attacks are interconnected and can be interchanged in many situations. Again, we pick up the technique as Royce transitions from one side to the other after trapping Pedro's arm with his elbow on the mat and locking the arm.

1 Royce is transitioning from Pedro's left side to his right after having trapped the right arm with his right elbow. Royce starts the armlock attack by driving his left hand under Pedro's left arm. Royce grabs Pedro's left wrist with his right hand and wraps his left arm under Pedro's left arm until he locks his hand on his own right wrist for total arm control.

2 Opting for the Kimura, Royce traps Pedro's right arm by dropping his right knee on the ground over Pedro's right arm. This prevents Pedro from countering the Kimura by holding his left hand with the right one and keeps Pedro trapped under Royce.

3 Royce starts the Kimura as he gets his torso upright and torques Pedro's left arm up toward his own body. Royce makes sure he lifts Pedro's hand up so Pedro can't grip the belt or his gi on the way back to block the move. (See next page for how to proceed if your opponent does manage to grab his belt.)

4 Royce twists his upper body to his left, torquing Pedro's arm toward his back, forcing the shoulder joint for the submission.

Breaking the opponent's grip if he grabs his belt: Many times when faced with a Kimura, the opponent will hold his own belt to keep the attacker from pulling his arm out. Royce shows how to break the grip.

1 In blocking the Kimura, Pedro was able to grab his own belt to defend the submission. Should Royce try to simply pull Pedro's arm up from here, it would be very difficult; Pedro's grip is very strong in the upward direction.

2 Instead, Royce twists his entire torso to his own right, pulling Pedro's left wrist away from the belt, not up. This forces the belt to slip through the opening between Pedro's fingers and his thumb.

3 Royce torques his body to his left, making sure Pedro's hand is far away from his torso so he cannot grab the belt again.

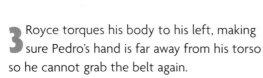

59. Side-control transition attack 4: armlock—opponent blocks the transition

When faced with an imminent armlock from the side-control transition, many opponents will trap the attacker's arms to prevent the move. Royce demonstrates how to alter the regular motion slightly and proceed with a variation of the regular armlock.

1 Royce has side-control on Pedro and is transitioning from one side to the other. In the transition he is able to trap Pedro's arm by sliding his left arm under Pedro's. Should Pedro allow Royce to continue, he would be submitted via armlock.

2 Pedro counters Royce's attack by using his right arm to grab Royce's right arm in an effort to keep Royce from moving.

3 Royce sits on the mat and swings his right leg around over Pedro's head. At the same time, he uses his right hand under Pedro's triceps to pull the arm up with him. Notice how low Royce is compared to a regular armlock move.

4 Royce continues to lean back, pulling Pedro's right arm with him. Pedro grabs his right biceps with the left hand to keep Royce from extending the arm, making it even more difficult to execute the armlock. Royce slides his left knee over Pedro's left torso.

5 Royce loops his left leg over as he continues to pull Pedro by the right arm.

6 Royce leans back as he pulls Pedro's right elbow open toward his right shoulder, breaking the grip and extending the left arm for the armlock.

60. Side-control transition attack 5: knee-slide to Kimura

Many times when you use the knee-slide method to achieve the mount, your opponent will try to block the move by pushing your knee with his outside hand. Royce takes advantage of the common defense and goes for a Kimura.

1 Royce attempts to reach the mount using the knee-slide method, sliding his right knee over Pedro's stomach. Pedro uses his left hand to push Royce's knee in an attempt to block the move. When Pedro pushes against Royce's knee, his arm leaves a gap between his elbow and torso. Royce takes advantage of that and attacks the arm.

2 Royce coils his arm back . . .

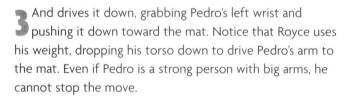

3 And drives it down, grabbing Pedro's left wrist and pushing it down toward the mat. Notice that Royce uses his weight, dropping his torso down to drive Pedro's arm to the mat. Even if Pedro is a strong person with big arms, he cannot stop the move.

4 Royce slides his left arm under Pedro's elbow and locks his left hand on his own right, completing the figure-four lock necessary for the Kimura.

5 Royce steps out with his left leg so that the knee is up and slides his right knee forward, switching the hips.

6 Royce walks his left leg until the foot is on the opposite side of Pedro's head. Notice that Royce maintains his weight on Pedro's arm, keeping it pinned to the mat.

7 Pushing off his left foot, Royce leans to his right as he lifts Pedro's elbow and drives Pedro's wrist in the opposite direction, twisting Pedro's arm around the shoulder for the Kimura.

61. Side-control to mount 11: S-mount

The S-mount is a dynamic and surprising way to achieve the mount. Opportunities to use the S-mount occur when transitioning from side to side in side-control, or the mount may be set up with a hip switch and an apparent attack on the near arm. With the opponent's attention directed to defending that arm, a quick swing of the leg and presto, you are mounted!

1 Royce is across-side on Pedro.

2 Royce switches his hips, planting his left foot out and sliding his right knee under as he grabs Pedro's right arm with his left arm, showing some interest in the arm.

3 Royce continues sliding his right leg under until his hips are facing Pedro's head. Royce continues pulling on Pedro's right arm to keep Pedro's attention on the arm.

4 Royce places his right hand on the mat next to Pedro's left hip and pushes off his left foot, sliding his right hip on top of Pedro's stomach. Notice how Royce pulls Pedro's right arm up with him. At this point, Royce's weight should be on his right buttock on top of Pedro's ribcage. His right arm is on the mat, allowing him to pivot his body in any direction.

5 Pivoting off his right buttock and arm, Royce lets go of Pedro's right arm as he spins his right leg around over Pedro's head until his heel touches the mat on Pedro's left side. Royce drives his hips forward, trapping Pedro's right arm.

6 Royce adjusts his legs so his knees touch the ground, achieving the mount.

62. Side-control transition attack 6: S-mount to triangle

An opportunity for the triangle occurs during the S-mount. It is a natural continuation: The leg swings and usually ends up on top of the opponent's opposite arm with one arm inside. Royce demonstrates the proper way to achieve the submission from the S-mount.

1 Royce is swinging his right leg over Pedro's head for the S-mount.

2 Instead of swinging the leg all the way around until it is parallel to Pedro's stomach, Royce stops just as it passes over Pedro's head and drops his thigh over the top of Pedro's left shoulder. Royce pulls Pedro's right elbow with his left hand.

3 Royce curls his right leg back and pulls on Pedro's head with the right hand as he continues pulling Pedro's right arm with his left arm. Royce drives his hips up so that he locks Pedro's head and left arm with his legs and hips.

4 Royce leans back slightly and pulls Pedro's head and left arm up, allowing enough space for his right leg to circle under Pedro's head. At this point Pedro's arm and head are completely trapped.

5 Royce leans to his right, pulling Pedro's right arm toward his left to help lock his legs in a figure-four.

6 Royce locks his right foot behind his left knee for the figure-four triangle.

7 Royce pulls on Pedro's head with his left arm as he squeezes his legs for the triangle choke.

8 As an option, Royce may swing his left arm around Pedro's right arm, trapping it under his armpit and applying an arm bar by leaning back with his left shoulder.

ATTACKING THE TURTLE

One of the most common escapes from the side-control position is for the opponent to turn onto his knees, reaching the all-fours or turtle position. You see this a lot in street fights as well as refereed matches. The key to controlling and attacking the turtle is to maintain pressure with your chest on the opponent's back and shift your body position in relation to his body, not allowing him to turn back to the guard or escape by standing up or, worse, sliding to your back. Still, the turtle position provides one of the best opportunities to strike your opponent. Always consider the possibility to, without releasing your pressure, deliver knee strikes to your opponent's head and side.

63. Attacking the turtle 1: clock choke

Many times when you are in side-control, your opponent will escape by turning to his knees, reaching the turtle position. When that happens it is the perfect opportunity to use the clock choke. In many cases Royce allows the opponent to begin his escape, which opens up submissions via the clock choke. The key to this attack is the set up, with the hand going deep in the lapel early but not too tight, so you don't alert the opponent of the imminent danger.

1 Royce has across-side position on Pedro. Royce has his left elbow tight against the left side of Pedro's head, keeping him from moving his head. Royce's chest presses against Pedro's chest, preventing him from initiating an escape.

2 Royce brings his knees in and gives a little space between his chest and Pedro's chest, allowing Pedro to start his escape. Pedro escapes his hips to his left and starts turning into Royce to go to the turtle position.

3 Royce grabs Pedro's right lapel with his left hand as close to the back of the neck as possible. Royce does not tighten the pressure on Pedro's neck; otherwise Pedro would sense the danger and turn back to his left, placing his back on the mat and stopping the attack.

4 Royce continues to allow Pedro to turn toward him. He places his right hand on the mat for balance and gives Pedro even more space between their bodies.

5 As Pedro starts to reach his knees, he is in perfect position for the clock choke. At this point there is already some pressure from the top blade of Royce's forearm against Pedro's neck. Royce does not want to let Pedro turn back and place his back on the mat to release the pressure, so Royce presses down with his chest on Pedro's left shoulder, preventing him from going back. Royce may also use his right hand to grab Pedro's right hip, blocking him from turning back.

6 Royce grapevines his right arm inside Pedro's right arm, grabbing the wrist with his right hand. Royce has complete control over Pedro. Pedro cannot continue to turn in, as he would simply choke himself, and he cannot turn to his left and place his back on the mat, as Royce controls his right side as well as pressuring his back.

7 Royce opens his left leg and plants his foot forward in front of Pedro's head while still pressing down with his chest on Pedro's back.

8 Royce completes the clock choke by sliding his right leg forward so that the weight of his body hangs down, pressing with his chest against Pedro's left shoulder as he pulls Pedro's lapel up with his left hand. Royce can add more pressure by "walking" forward, applying even more pressure with his chest down on Pedro's shoulder while tightening the noose on the collar with his left hand.

64. Attacking the turtle 2: clock-choke variation

A common defensive maneuver to counter the clock choke is for the opponent to place both hands on the ground, push his chest up, and try to sit back so his back touches the mat, taking away the choking pressure. Of course, this shouldn't happen if you properly maintain your weight as you execute the clock choke, but in the real world, many times your opponent reacts quickly or is extremely strong, or you simply did not maintain the proper weight on his back at all times. Nevertheless, when this occurs there is a great technique that will solve the problem.

1 Royce is attempting a clock choke on Pedro, but Pedro is able to plant both hands on the ground and is pushing up, trying to sit back and replace the guard. Royce may continue trying the clock choke but he may also lose the position.

2 Instead, Royce steps back with his right foot so that his chest is perpendicular and square on top of Pedro's back. Notice that Royce maintains his grip on the collar and on Pedro's right wrist.

3 Royce steps in with his right knee just under Pedro's left armpit and hooks Pedro's left arm with his left leg.

4 Royce extends his left leg back, driving Pedro's left arm back with it as he crosses over his right knee. At this point, Royce can either apply the armlock by driving his hips down against Pedro's left elbow, hyperextending it, or he can use a choke variation.

5 Royce goes for the collar choke, releasing his right hand from Pedro's right wrist and grabbing the left lapel with it. Royce applies the choke by pulling on both lapels.

6 *Detail* Notice that Royce reaches with his right arm under Pedro's arm and grabs the left lapel with his hand. Royce applies the choking pressure by pulling up with his left hand and extending the right arm, tightening the choke around Pedro's neck.

65. Attacking the turtle 3: crucifix

Another effective option when your opponent is pushing up to escape the clock choke is the crucifix. The entire setup is very similar to the one in technique 64, except that Royce rolls over his shoulder, bringing Pedro over with him, instead of controlling the arm and applying his weight on the back for the collar choke. Both options are very effective; which you use is just a matter of personal preference. The crucifix is an especially good option when you are going for the armlock but the opponent turns his wrist in and is able to bend his arm and bring his forearm forward, defending the elbow joint. We pick up the position after Royce has hooked Pedro's arm.

1 Royce has hooked Pedro's left arm with his left leg and is attempting an armlock by pushing his hips against Pedro's left elbow. He may also be going for the collar choke.

2 Pedro is able to turn his left wrist and bend the arm forward to release the pressure on the elbow.

3 Royce pushes off his left hand and rolls forward over his right shoulder as he kicks his left leg over, bringing Pedro around with him.

4 As Royce continues to roll over, he makes sure his leg is hooked and pressing against Pedro's arm to keep him from escaping. At this point, Royce is looking to grab Pedro's right collar with his left hand. Notice that Royce has released the right-hand grip on Pedro's right wrist and extends the right hand toward his own head.

5 At the end of the roll, Royce has his left hand gripping Pedro's right collar, his legs are trapping Pedro's left arm, and his right arm is trapping Pedro's right arm as he reaches the back of his head with the palm of his right hand. Royce applies the choke by pulling down Pedro's collar with the left hand.

66. Attacking the turtle 4: reaching side-control

One of the most important things one can do when faced with an opponent that has a good turtle position is to get side-control on him. The person in the turtle can close himself very well, with knees and elbows so tight that you cannot find any openings for attacks. Should you fail to bring him back to side-control, the match may end or he may roll over and replace the guard. Royce shows a clever and effective way to get your opponent from the turtle back to your side-control.

1 Pedro is in the turtle position and Royce attempts to attack. Pedro has closed himself very well, elbows tight against his thighs, leaving no space for Royce to attack. Notice Royce's weight distribution. Although he does not see an opening, Royce does not want to allow Pedro the opportunity to stand up or roll over and replace the guard, so he has his legs spread and pushes off both feet, pressing his chest against Pedro's back. Notice that Royce's head is not hanging over Pedro's back; otherwise, he would be off balance and Pedro could easily roll him over and end up on top.

2 Royce brings his right knee to the mat, placing it against Pedro's left leg toward the ankle. By doing this, Royce locks Pedro's leg, preventing him from opening it up for a brace. With his right hand, Royce will hook Pedro's right hip, while his left hand pushes against Pedro's left hip.

2 *Detail* Notice how Royce hooks his right hand on Pedro's right hip.

3 Royce leans toward his left as he pulls Pedro over with his right hand on the right hip. He may have to walk to his own left as he pulls Pedro over until his back is on the mat. Royce uses his left hand to brace and to help him move to his left. Pedro cannot open his left leg to brace, as it is still being blocked by Royce's right knee, so Pedro is forced to roll over.

4 Royce continues pulling Pedro by the right hip until his back is on the mat and he ends up in side-control.

67. Attacking the turtle 5: taking the back as the opponent turns

Since it is so common for opponents to turn turtle as an escape from side-control or as a way to defend the guard pass, anticipating it happening will give you a great edge in securing good positions and submissions. Royce demonstrates a great technique to take advantage of the opponent's attempt to turn turtle. This is such an effective move that if mastered you are actually going to allow your opponent to roll in order to take his back. Here, Royce uses a similar hook as in the previous position to control the speed and ability of Pedro to turn turtle. By practicing this position until mastered you will have a formidable weapon in your arsenal.

1 Royce has side-control on Pedro, or may have just reached Pedro's side after passing the guard. Pedro has his arms tight in front of him and is getting ready to turn to his left and reach the turtle position.

2 *Alternate angle* As Pedro starts his rotation to his left by throwing his right leg over the left, Royce hooks his right hand on Pedro's right hip and opens his right leg, planting his right foot on the mat. With his right hand on Pedro's hip, Royce can control the speed of Pedro's rotation, making it easy for him to apply the technique. Notice that Royce can lean back and prevent Pedro from going to his knees altogether, or at least delay the roll.

3 Pulling himself forward by the right arm hooked against Pedro's hip, Royce slides his left leg on the mat and hooks the left foot inside Pedro's left leg. Since Royce controls Pedro's rotation with the right arm, Royce can actually take his time reaching the hook. The movement is as if Royce were diving under Pedro's body.

4 Still in control over Pedro's rotation, Royce pulls himself over Pedro's back by the right hand as he throws his right leg over.

5 Royce hooks his right leg on Pedro's right leg. Since the left leg was already inside Pedro's left leg, the hook occurs almost naturally and Royce is on Pedro's back.

68. Attacking the turtle 6: head-and-arm choke

Many times when your opponent is in the turtle position he will grab one or both of your legs in an attempt to either replace the guard or pull you down, reversing the position and putting your back on the mat. Royce has a very solid choke ready for just such an occasion. This technique can also be used as a defense for the single-leg take-down if you manage to sprawl and get your knee on the mat.

1 Pedro grabs Royce's right leg from the turtle position. Should Royce allow it, Pedro would pull Royce's leg in toward Royce's left and force him to the mat, achieving the top position. Royce counters by pushing down on Pedro's back with his arms, keeping distance and defending the reversal.

2 Royce slides his right arm next to the left side of Pedro's head, reaching with his right hand until it comes out under Pedro's right armpit. At the same time, he uses his left hand to push Pedro's right arm in slightly. Royce makes sure the top blade of his forearm presses against Pedro's throat, while dropping his chest and pressing down on Pedro's back to keep him locked.

2 *Reverse angle* Notice how Royce slides his right arm next to the left side of Pedro's head. It is very important to drive the arm through and tight against the neck; otherwise, it may not stick out enough on the other side for you to grab your biceps.

3 Royce locks his right hand on his left biceps and reaches with his left arm until his hand rests on Pedro's back. At this point, Royce has trapped Pedro's right arm and neck inside his lock. At the same time, Royce drops his left knee to the mat.

4 Royce rolls over his left shoulder, forcing Pedro to roll with him. Should Pedro resist, he will choke himself on Royce's right forearm, which is pushing against his throat.

5 Royce ends up under Pedro and cinches the choke by pulling his forearm tight against his chest.

KNEE-ON-STOMACH

The knee-on-stomach is a very effective position in jiu-jitsu. It is a good position to deliver strikes in an NHB match and it opens many options for attacking in both NHB and jiu-jitsu matches. The pressure of the knee pushing down on the opponent's stomach not only induces him to hastily react, looking for an escape, but it also works to undermine his resistance, much like a boxer strikes the midsection to wear down his opponent. The constant pressure of the knee-on-stomach will wear down even the most fit opponent. With the proper posture—the head held high—the knee-on-stomach allows for great vision of the situation and the opponent's reactions. It is very important to remain nimble and ready to react to any changes in his position. One of the ways to add pressure and remain nimble is to have your weight on your knee, making your opponent uncomfortable, and not on the toes of the leg that applies the knee-on-stomach. Your toes should be either off the ground or just lightly touching the ground; that way, not only do you ensure that most of your weight is on the knee against the opponent's stomach, but also you can quickly react by either pivoting on your knee or shifting your weight to the open leg.

It is also important when maintaining the knee-on-stomach to keep proper distance between your chest and the opponent's chest, both for posture and to prevent the opponent from grabbing your collar to pull you down off base.

69. Knee-on-stomach 1: parallel collar choke

The choke is one of the most effective and common attacks from the knee-on-stomach position. Controlling the opponent with the knee-on-stomach leads him to worry so much about escaping the uncomfortable situation that he will forget to defend the collar attack. The most common of the chokes is the regular cross-choke, where you grip the opposite collar with each hand and choke by pulling the collar to your chest while pulling your elbows back. Since this is a common and recognizable attack, the defender will key on the first hand grip and struggle even more to escape the position. To avoid that, come in with the right hand gripping the left collar (same side of the body) in a seemingly innocuous grip that the opponent will not worry about until it is too late.

1 Royce starts across-side on Pedro. He plants both hands on the ground or on Pedro's chest and props himself up to the classic knee-on-stomach position, with the right knee on Pedro's stomach and the left leg opened out, foot solidly planted on the mat and knee slightly bent, pointing up.

2 Keeping both arms straight, Royce slides his right hand with the palm facing up inside Pedro's left collar and slides his left hand with the palm facing down inside Pedro's right collar. Since both arms are parallel, Pedro does not feel any immediate sense of danger.

3 Royce drops down from knee-on-stomach to side-control and applies the choke by bending both arms, bringing the forearms together while driving his right elbow to the mat. He pushes his forearm against Pedro's throat while keeping his left forearm perpendicular to the mat against Pedro's neck. Should Royce need to further tighten the choke, he would move in a clockwise direction toward Pedro's head for the north-south position. *Warning:* One of the biggest mistakes done in executing this choke is to drop your left elbow to the mat as well. Even the slightest deviation from perpendicular to the mat will yield some space and loosen up the choke. It is imperative to have the left forearm perpendicular to the mat against the defender's neck.

70. Knee-on-stomach 2: armlock

A common way to escape the knee-on-stomach and the discomfort it causes is for the defender to use his outside hand to push the knee away from his stomach. Many times when doing that, the defender will leave his elbow open and away from the body, exposing the space for an armlock. Note that in this case Royce can either go for the regular armlock, as he demonstrates here, or go for the Kimura, in which case he would use his right hand to lock Pedro's left wrist and would grapevine his left arm around Pedro's left arm, locking the left hand on his own right wrist for the typical Kimura lock, and apply pressure to the shoulder as demonstrated in technique 60, Side-control transition attack 5: knee-slide to Kimura.

1 Royce has knee-on-stomach on Pedro with his right knee across Pedro's belly. Pedro uses his left arm to push Royce's knee back in an attempt to escape the position or simply to relieve the pressure on his stomach. Notice that Pedro has his left elbow slightly away from his ribs, creating a space for Royce to explore.

2 Royce slides his right hand with the palm facing out inside the gap between Pedro's left elbow and chest and pulls the elbow up toward himself, turning Pedro over to his right.

3 While still pulling up on Pedro's left elbow with his right hand, Royce plants his right toes on the mat, pivots on his right knee, and spins around Pedro's head, planting his left foot on Pedro's left side slightly past the shoulder. Notice that Royce's right foot remained on Pedro's right side near the head in perfect position for the armlock. Royce does not step over with the right foot, but rather pivots on it as well.

4 Royce sits on the mat, pivots on his left toes so that his left knee touches the left side of Pedro's ribcage, and pulls Pedro's left arm with him for the armlock. It is important throughout the entire movement for Royce to keep pulling up on Pedro's left elbow to maintain control of it and keep Pedro from turning to his left and yanking it out.

5 Royce drops his head to the mat as he extends Pedro's arm and hyperextends the elbow for the armlock by driving his hips up. Notice that Royce controls Pedro's arm with his left hand on the wrist and right hand on the elbow, preventing Pedro from twisting the elbow away from the pressure.

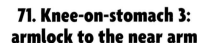

71. Knee-on-stomach 3: armlock to the near arm

Another classic stance for the knee-on-stomach is for the attacker to prop himself in the position while controlling the near arm by the wrist or gi sleeve and pulling it. In some cases the opponent actually attempts to escape the knee-on-stomach by using the near arm to push the attacker's hips, extending it. Whenever this occurs, regardless of why, the armlock to the near arm is a great submission option.

1 Royce has knee-on-stomach with his right knee on Pedro's belly. Pedro's right arm is extended. He is either using it to push Royce's hips away to escape the position, or Royce simply has control of the sleeve and has pulled it up. Regardless, the armlock option is present.

2 Royce braces his right hand on Pedro's chest, leaning over Pedro's body, and pushes off his left foot, extending the leg as he pulls up on Pedro's right arm, turning Pedro to his left and bringing Royce's hips close to Pedro's right elbow. Notice Royce's straight line with his left leg and body. This is very important to maintain base and execute the next step.

3 Keeping his head up, Royce steps around Pedro's head with his left leg until his foot lands on the left side of Pedro's head. Notice that Royce does not step over Pedro's head, because he would lose his balance. Instead, he does a semicircle with his left foot around Pedro's head. Royce pulls up on Pedro's right arm the entire time. The more he pulls up on the arm, the more he turns Pedro over toward his left shoulder, making it a shorter path for the foot to circle over the head and therefore making it easier for Royce to armlock him.

4 Royce sits back toward the mat. He brings his knees in and uses his right hand to pull up on Pedro's left elbow while still keeping Pedro's left arm extended and under control.

5 Royce leans back with his torso as he pulls Pedro's right arm with him for the armlock.

MAINTAINING THE MOUNT

Attaining the mount in a fight should be tantamount to winning the fight. In sports competition you are awarded four points for the mount. In NHB and street fighting, it is such a dominant position that you should be able to finish the fight with strikes. However, the mount can be a very unstable position if one does not master the counters to it. Many practitioners fail to fully understand the position, don't practice maintaining it, and end up letting their opponent escape. Like everything else, practice and repetition makes perfect. Practice these drills and techniques and your mount will be the envy of your friends and the terror of your opponents.

Correct posture

The correct posture for the mount is shown here. Royce's arms are next to his body and his hands are ready to grab Gui's collar for a choke or arms for a key-lock, a Kimura, or even to set up an armlock. Notice that Royce has his feet tucked in near Gui's hips. His knees are tight against the chest and Royce is NOT sitting on Gui. Sitting on your opponent makes you slower in countering any defensive movement. As Royce likes to say, "Your opponent is not a chair!"

Incorrect posture

Notice how Royce's legs and feet are open and he is sitting on Gui. His feet position will impede Royce from quickly turning to one of his knees for a side-mount as a counter to Gui turning to his side for an elbow escape. In addition, Royce's knees are away from Gui's side, making it easier for Gui to initiate the elbow escape. Royce's left hand is on Gui's chest, making it easy for Gui to trap it.

The next techniques are shown as drills because they can and should be repeated alone or in conjunction with each other as ways to maintain the mount. Each is a counter to an escape, so drill and master each of them separately, then combine them for an extremely powerful drill.

72. Maintaining the mount 1: swimming

One of the most common ways for a beginner to remove someone from the mount is by pushing. Although a skilled fighter has many options to counter and even attack from a push (armlock, Kimura), surprisingly enough the push can be a very effective escape if you are not prepared to deal with it. In this first drill, Royce demonstrates how to deal with a push using a technique called swimming. Notice that Royce does not fight with Gui's arm pressure, but rather "swims" inside it, deflecting the push. After some time, Gui will either give up or end up submitted by an armlock or punches rained on him.

1 Royce begins the drill mounted on Gui. He leans forward, putting his hands on Gui's shoulders.

2 Gui extends his arms and pushes Royce's chest away.

3 Royce turns his torso as he brings his left shoulder back and his right one forward, deflecting Gui's push pressure. At the same time, he brings his right hand in and slides it inside Gui's left arm.

4 Royce drops his weight forward until his right hand hits the mat. Royce remains very fluid and loose, with his shoulder and upper chest deflecting any power that Gui's arms may have. Once his right hand is on the mat, Royce circles his left hand inside Gui's right arm. Notice Royce's hands: All five fingers together like a blade so they can easily slide between the narrow gap.

5 Royce opens his left arm and plants the hand on the ground after he "swims" inside Gui's arms.

6 Repeat the drill several times, alternating which arm comes in first. It is extremely important to keep your chest loose; otherwise, you allow the push to be effective against your stiff upper body.

73. Maintaining the mount 2: low-push deflection

Another effective escape from the bottom is for the person to push against your hips. This escape is used even by experienced grapplers with great success. If one is not prepared to properly react to it, the person on the bottom will simply maintain the pressure and slide his hips back and out for an elbow escape or similar escape. Again, Royce's jiu-jitsu is based not on force but on reaction. Instead of fighting against the pressure on the hips, Royce drives his hips forward, deflecting Gui's arms and the pressure.

1 Royce is mounted on Gui, but Gui has both his hands locked on Royce's hips, pushing them away. Notice that Gui can push away or to the sides, forcing Royce off to one side and escaping his hips to the opposite side to escape from the mount.

2 Royce drives his hips forward, deflecting Gui's hands off his hips. To do so, Royce extended his body, pushing off his knees and arching his head back as he raised his hips off Gui. Notice how Royce's body is straight, his hips thrusting forward and his shoulders and head leaning back.

3 With his hips still forward, Royce turns his shoulders to his left and pushes Gui's left hand from his hips with his right hand. Since Gui has no pressure against the hips, his arm is easily swayed.

4 Royce turns his shoulders back and deflects Gui's right hand off his hips.

5 Royce leans forward and puts his hands on the mat as he uses his chest to trap Gui's arms.

74. Maintaining the mount 3: low-push deflection (late reaction)

We can't all react as quickly as Royce. Sometimes you will be late with the low-push reaction demonstrated in technique 73 and your opponent will lock his arms on your hips and successfully push them away. When that happens, and you cannot drive your hips forward anymore, opt for this counter instead.

1 Gui defends by pushing against Royce's hips with his arms. This time Royce is late in his reaction and Gui succeeds in pushing the hips back and away.

2 Royce uses another option to counter. He leans forward and wraps his right arm around Gui's head, locking his chest against Gui's and making it very difficult for Gui to escape his hips and drive his torso away from Royce to escape the mount.

3 To complete the control, Royce grapevines his legs around Gui's legs. Notice how Royce hooks his legs inside Gui's legs. Once he does that, he drives his hips down against Gui's hips, taking away any possibility of an escape.

75. Maintaining the mount 4: knee-push deflection

The knee push is another escape from the mount you sometimes encounter. In it, the defender pushes the attacker's knee, slides his hips away from that knee, and replaces the guard. Again, Royce does not fight the force but rather deflects it. When you practice this drill, your partner should alternate pushing against each knee, and you should pull and deflect the pressure. After a few repetitions, ride your knees up for the high mount.

1 Royce is mounted on Gui and Gui begins his escape by pushing Royce's left knee with his right hand.

2 Rather than trying to push his knee back against Gui's arm, Royce cups his left hand under Gui's right wrist.

3 Royce simply pulls up the wrist, releasing the pressure against the knee.

4 Taking advantage of the control over Gui's right arm, Royce pulls the arm up and slides his left knee up, locking it just under Gui's right armpit.

5 Royce repeats the same motion on the right side, ending up with his knees against Gui's armpits in the high mount, dominating Gui's arms.

76. Maintaining the mount 5: opponent sits up

Another surprisingly effective escape from the mount is for the defender to plant his hands on the ground and sit up to one side, rolling the attacker to the side. Although it appears too simple to be effective, it actually works, especially if the person in the mount is sitting on his opponent or leans back for some reason. Here, Royce demonstrates the proper reaction.

1 Royce is sitting back in the mount on top of Gui. Although sitting is not proper posture for the mount, many times in a street fight or in a match, your opponent's scramble forces you to temporarily assume an incorrect position. Gui plants his hands back on the mat and sits forward, turning his torso toward his left.

2 Royce drives his right arm into Gui's face, blocking him from moving forward and forcing him back. At the same time, Royce wraps his left hand around Gui's right elbow.

3 Royce pulls Gui's right elbow open. Notice that Royce doesn't pull against the elbow, but rather pulls it open in a circular motion, forcing it forward. Gui has to release the hand on the ground. Should he resist this, he will injure his shoulder as his arm torques, pivoting on the right hand planted on the ground.

4 Royce pulls up on Gui's right arm as he turns to his left and drives his own right arm against Gui's face, forcing him back to the ground.

5 Royce ends up with his head on Gui's right side, having forced him back to the ground and thwarted the attempted escape.

77. Maintaining the mount 6: opponent rolls to one side

Beginners often react to being mounted by rolling to one side. Royce allows Gui to roll over, preferably all the way to his back, setting up a possible rear naked choke or a barrage of strikes to the back of the head. It is very important to learn to react to this move. Many beginners tend to lock their knees tight in an attempt to prevent the opponent from rolling, however, should Royce clamp his knees against Gui to lock him in place, he may end up rolling with him or having Gui simply force the leg open and slide out. It's much better to follow the defender's motion, as Royce demonstrates.

1 Royce is mounted on Gui.

2 Gui begins to roll to his left. Royce plants his left hand on the ground and slightly opens his knees, allowing enough space for Gui to roll.

3 With both hands on the ground, Royce follows Gui as he rolls to the left, keeping his body always centered on top of Gui's body.

4 Gui rolls all the way to his back with Royce still centered and mounted on him. From this position, Royce has full control over the situation and has many choices, such as a choke or strikes to the head.

5 Continue the drill by having your opponent roll to either side and even change directions. Make sure you walk your hands on the ground to keep your body centered and above his at all times.

6 *Incorrect technique* Gui rolls to his left and Royce locks his legs tight against Gui's body, losing his balance and rolling to his own right, ending up with Gui in his guard after losing the mount.

7 *Detail* Notice how Gui's left knee naturally locks Royce's right ankle and leg, preventing him from opening it up and blocking the roll.

78. Maintaining the mount 7: opponent bear hugs

A very common defense for a person being mounted is to wrap his arms around your waist in a bear hug. This is especially common when you grapevine your legs around your opponent's legs in order to maintain the mount. Although the bear hug is not really an escape, but more of a stalling technique, being able to break it and proceed to a submission is important—especially if you are in a timed match and your opponent is trying to run out the clock.

1 Royce is mounted on Gui with his legs grapevined around Gui's legs and his hips pushing forward and down against Gui's hips, locking him in place.

2 Royce pushes off his arms to create space between his chest and Gui's chest so he can attack or deliver strikes. As he can't escape, Gui bear hugs Royce's waist in an attempt to stall the match or to keep Royce from raising his chest and achieving a good distance for position.

3 Royce braces off his left arm and circles his right arm around Gui's head, bringing it close to his chest in order to pry Gui's face away.

4 Royce slides his arm down his chest, locking the blade of the arm against Gui's face.

5 Royce's forearm forms a frame against Gui's face and he is able to create some space between Gui's face and his chest.

6 Royce grabs his right wrist with his left hand, creating a very solid frame. Royce locks the frame against Gui's face and pries his chest away from Gui as he breaks the bear hug by driving his right elbow against Gui's jaw.

6 *Detail* Notice Royce's frame pushing against Gui's jaw.

7 Royce continues to put pressure against Gui's jaw, forcing him to break the bear hug and use his arms to push away Royce's frame to relieve the pressure.

79. Maintaining the mount 8: opponent bear hugs (variation with armlock)

Another option to deal with the bear hug in the mount is presented here. This time Royce not only breaks the bear hug but sets himself up for a series of submissions. This is a good option for those who have good hip flexibility; it may not work so well for someone who has difficulty bringing the leg around. If that is you, use the previous technique.

1 Royce is mounted on Gui and Gui bear hugs him.

2 Royce plants his arms on the mat and leans forward as he slides his left foot around and forward and stretches his leg, planting his left foot above Gui's head. Notice that at this point Royce has trapped Gui's right arm between his left arm and leg in the crease of his left hip.

3 Royce then brings his right leg around and forward in the same manner. At this point Royce is sitting on Gui's chest, applying a great deal of pressure. Notice how Royce has his torso and head leaning forward to keep his balance. Should he try to have his torso upright, he would actually be vulnerable to fall back, as his legs are forward and he has nothing to brace with. From this position, Royce can take either arm for an armlock.

4 Royce breaks the bear hug by driving one of his arms, in this case the left one, against Gui's neck. Royce plants his left hand on Gui's right shoulder, driving the blade of his forearm against Gui's throat, forcing him to release the bear hug or be choked.

5 As he breaks the bear hug, Royce slides his right elbow on his thigh until he traps Gui's left arm with his right armpit.

6 Royce brings his right knee in and leans slightly to his right, applying pressure to Gui's elbow for the submission. Note that Royce can go for a regular armlock, falling to the side on either arm just as well. To do that, all he has to do is circle either leg around Gui's head, moving his hips to the side of the arm he wants to armlock.

6 *Detail* Notice how Royce brings his right knee in and drives his shoulder to his right, applying pressure to Gui's left elbow. It is very important for Royce to keep his arm tight against Gui's arm as he performs this move; otherwise, Gui can just pull his arm out. As a way to add pressure, Royce can slide his right foot slightly back to help drive his knee against the elbow.

80. Maintaining the mount 9: Opponent hugs the neck

A common, though ineffective, way to deal with the mount is for the defender to hug the neck of the person mounted on him. Being able to escape a neck grab like this is important, especially in a street fight against a larger opponent, who can make you extremely uncomfortable by squeezing your neck. Royce uses leverage and weight to deal with the situation.

1 Royce is mounted on Gui, but Gui grabs around Royce's neck with his arms.

2 Royce plants both arms on the mat to prevent Gui from rolling him over to his left. He then advances the leg on the same side as the arm that is wrapped around his neck. In this case it is the right arm, so Royce advances his left knee until it is close to Gui's head. Royce plants his right heel next to Gui's hips, taking away any space for the hip to move. Notice that Royce's right knee is up for balance and mobility. At this point, Royce has a firm base in all directions. It is very important for him to maintain base at all times; otherwise, Gui can roll him over and be on top with a neck crank.

3 Royce makes a frame in front of Gui's face, with the blade of his left arm pushing against Gui's jaw and the right hand clasping the left wrist. Note that Royce's escape does not involve pushing off the frame and prying his head up and out; that would be very hard against a strong opponent and Royce would end up hurting his own neck.

4 Instead, Royce drives his weight forward, putting all the pressure on the frame, forcing his left arm against Gui's jaw. Again, note that Royce is not trying to push his head up and away, but rather puts all his weight on the frame against Gui's jaw.

5 With such tremendous pressure on the jaw, Gui has no recourse and releases the grip. Notice that Gui's arm is trapped and Royce is in perfect position for an armlock, should he decide to apply one.

ATTACKING FROM THE MOUNT

Once you have mastered a variety of situations and drills designed to maintain the mount, you can proceed to learn a series of submissions from the mount. The mount provides the ideal angle to deliver a variety of striking, choking, and joint-locking techniques. It is extremely important, however, for you to learn to maintain the mount first. Many times fighters are so eager to submit an opponent that they forget about maintaining the position and end up losing the mount. The opponent replaces the guard or, worse, you end up on the bottom with the opponent in your guard.

The fact of the matter is that by maintaining the mount and countering your opponent's efforts to escape, you force your opponent to open up, giving you opportunities for submissions. If your opponent feels trapped under you, he is much more likely to try a desperate escape, exposing his neck and arms for chokes and locks. Also, if you are confident of your ability to maintain the position, you can be a lot more deliberate about going for submissions; you can take your time and wait for the right opportunities without feeling like your opponent may escape at any time.

81. Ezekiel choke

An often overlooked attack from the mount is the Ezekiel choke. Attackers are hesitant to use the Ezekiel because they feel like they may lose the mount; their arms are tied up in the choking process and they feel vulnerable to being rolled over with a bridge from the opponent. If you feel that your opponent will roll you over *before* the choke is in place, let go of everything, release the grip, open your arms, and plant your hands as wide as possible to stop the roll. If you feel the opponent is going to roll you *after* the choke is sunk, do not worry; continue the choking pressure and keep him in your closed guard as he rolls over. He will submit from the choke!

A good way to prevent the opponent from rolling you over when applying the Ezekiel is to grapevine your legs around his legs and drive your hips down, keeping him from being able to bridge up. The problem is that many times, as soon as you grapevine your legs around his, a savvy opponent will immediately defend his neck from the Ezekiel. To avoid that, you may instead set up the choke and then grapevine the legs as soon as the choke is in place.

1 Royce is mounted on Gui. Royce has proper position for an attack, especially the Ezekiel; his arms are opened with hands planted on both sides of Gui's head. His hips are down and forward.

2 To set up the choke, Royce wraps his left arm around Gui's head, making sure his hand is as far toward the opposite shoulder as possible to make it easy for the next step. Note that at this point Gui can grab Royce's left arm and bridge to his right for an escape. Royce is ready for that and can grapevine his legs around Gui's legs, or he may let go and open his left arm to stop the roll.

3 Royce brings his right arm closer to Gui's shoulder and grabs the inside of the sleeve with his left hand, with the four fingers on the inside and the thumb on the outside.

3 **Detail** Notice how Royce grabs the inside of the sleeve with his left hand: four fingers on the inside and the thumb on the outside.

4 Detail Notice how Royce uses his face to shield Gui from seeing the hand coming in for the choke. Also notice how he brings the right hand in with a closed fist until he is ready to open that palm for the choke.

4 Royce circles his right hand around in such a way that it ends up in front of Gui's neck. It is critical for Royce to try to circle the right hand as close to the left one as possible so that he doesn't alert Gui to the attack. Should he make a big loop with the hand around the head, Gui will sense the attack coming and will be more apt to counter it. Notice that Royce keeps his face close and to the left side of Gui's face, almost blocking his sight to the attack.

5 Having locked in the grip, Royce opens the right palm, forcing the blade of the hand against Gui's neck, while at the same time he extends the right arm and raises his chest away from Gui, applying a tremendous choking pressure on the neck for the submission.

5 *Detail* Notice the choking motion for the Ezekiel. Royce is still grabbing the inside of the right sleeve with his left hand and slides his right hand in front of Gui's neck.

5 *Front view* It would be incorrect for Royce to grab his left forearm with his right hand. Some practitioners make that mistake, taking away a lot of the pressure that the Ezekiel can deliver. Instead, Royce slides his right hand in front of the left forearm as he extends his arms for the added pressure. The motion of the choke should be like drawing a bow. Your left hand pulls the string and your right hand holds the bow.

82. Head-and-arm triangle

A great submission option from the mount is the head-and-arm triangle. Royce sets it up much as he would the double-attack or a choke or taking the back, making it difficult for Gui to recognize what attack is coming and therefore giving Royce an extra advantage. Remember that jiu-jitsu is a game of technique, timing, and quick thinking/reacting. Recognizing an impending attack gives the defender the edge and lack of recognition gives the attacker the edge.

1 Royce is mounted on Gui. He places his right hand on Gui's shoulder and drives his elbow down toward the mat, forcing the forearm down on Gui's throat. Royce shows the NHB version of the move, using the arm on the shoulder. In a jiu-jitsu tournament, he could opt for sliding the hand in the collar as if he were going for a regular collar choke. Gui reacts by using both hands to pull Royce's elbow up, releasing the pressure on his throat.

2 Royce pushes Gui's right elbow with his left hand, making sure to keep it from coming back toward the ground. Royce doesn't really need to push the elbow across but rather just brace to keep Gui from bringing it back to the ground.

3 Royce releases his right hand from Gui's shoulder, sliding it in front of Gui's head. At the same time, he drops his torso and head down toward Gui, locking Gui's right arm in place. Notice how Royce uses the right side of his head to lock Gui's right elbow and keep it from coming back to the ground.

4 Royce wraps his right arm around Gui's head while still maintaining his head pressing against Gui's right arm. This is a critical time; should Royce give Gui any space here, Gui would turn to his own right and try to put his right elbow on the ground to defend the head-and-arm triangle.

5 While still mounted on Gui, Royce grabs his left biceps with his right hand, locking the figure-four around Gui's head and right arm, and places his left forearm between Gui's head and his own head to add to the pressure. Royce can squeeze the choke from there on the mount by bringing his elbows together and driving his torso forward and his head in.

6 Sometimes the opponent will be able to resist the choke from the mount. If that happens, Royce will add additional pressure to the choke by stepping off to the same side as the trapped arm—in this case, the right arm.

7 Royce ends up across-side with the head-and-arm triangle locked in place. Royce squeezes his elbows together and drives his shoulders forward, crushing Gui's neck with tremendous choking pressure.

83. Head-and-arm triangle 2: opponent has elbows closed

Many times when a person is mounted he will assume very defensive postures, such as having the elbows closed next to the chest and the hands near the neck, protecting the choke. That is an extremely good defensive position, as the elbows will prevent the person on top from sliding his legs up and mounting higher against the chest for more power. Royce here not only demonstrates how to deal with the elbows closed, but also goes for a head-and-arm triangle submission.

1 Royce is mounted on Gui. Gui has very good defensive posture, with his elbows tight against his sides, blocking Royce from sliding up. Gui's hands protect his neck from any chokes.

2 Royce wraps his right arm around Gui's head as he turns his body back slightly toward his left . . .

3 And slides his left arm back until it locks inside Gui's right elbow. Now he is ready to pry the elbow open.

4 Royce "walks" his left hand forward like a caterpillar: reaching with the fingers out as far as they will go, planting them on the ground, and pulling the palm forward with the fingers. This drives Gui's elbow open. Royce follows Gui's elbow up with his left knee, driving it up as well.

5 At this point, Royce is perfectly set for the head-and-arm triangle shown in technique 82.

84. Triangle choke or armlock

Continuing from the same position achieved in the previous technique, Royce goes for more submission options like the regular triangle and an armlock.

1 Royce has Gui's right arm trapped. He could have reached this point by many methods, perhaps using technique 83, or perhaps he just ended up that way in a scramble. Gui still has his left elbow close to his torso for good posture and Royce has his right hand grabbing the back of Gui's head.

2 Royce climbs his right leg around and over Gui's left arm, placing his right knee as close to Gui's face as possible and locking Gui's right arm out of the way. Notice that Royce has his left hand planted on the ground for balance and has shifted his entire body in a counterclockwise direction on top of Gui to set up the attacks.

3 Royce shifts his weight to his left hand and lifts Gui's head, pulling it with his right hand as he circles his right leg around the head until it is under Gui's head.

4 Once his leg is under Gui's head, Royce drops his weight back down and his hands forward for balance. At this point, Gui's head and right arm are completely trapped by Royce's legs.

5 Pivoting off his right arm, Royce shifts his weight to the right and brings his left leg forward until it is ready to lock the figure-four. Royce uses his left hand to help lift his foot, easing the way to lock the triangle.

6 Royce re-centers his weight and applies the pressure by stretching his body, driving his hip forward and pulling Gui's head with both hands for the triangle choke.

7 Conversely, Royce can go for an armlock. He does so by sliding his left hand inside and around Gui's right arm (since that is the one trapped in the triangle).

8 Royce continues circling his arm around, trapping Gui's right arm and driving it back toward his hips.

9 Royce closes the knees together and applies an armlock by driving his left shoulder back, forcing Gui's elbow against his left thigh for the armlock. Notice that in this position Royce is in full control; if it was an NHB match he could rain punches down on a defenseless Gui.

85. Lapel choke 1

One of Royce's favorite options from the mount is the lapel choke. This is a position more useful in sport jiu-jitsu than in NHB matches, where the opponent doesn't wear a gi. The secret to this choke is to be sneaky and prepare the choke without alerting your opponent of your intentions. To accomplish this, Royce puts his face down and over Gui's face to block him from seeing the development of the move.

1 Royce is mounted on Gui. He has his right arm wrapped around Gui's head and his left arm planted on the ground. To set up the lapel choke, Royce brings his head down to the right side of Gui's face, blocking his sight.

2 With his left hand, Royce opens his left lapel as close to the end as possible. Royce makes sure he does this discreetly so as not to alert Gui.

3 Royce changes the arm that is wrapped around Gui's head. With his left hand, Royce drives the left lapel under Gui's head, plants his right hand on the mat . . .

4 And feeds the lapel to his right hand. Notice how Royce grabs the lapel with his palm facing up and the thumb at the far end of the lapel. As he grabs the lapel with the right hand, Royce changes the support arm and has his left forearm on the mat for base.

5 Royce leans to his left and stretches the lapel toward the right with his right hand. By leaning to his left, Royce allows more cloth to be pulled to the right side and cinches the collar around the left side of Gui's neck.

6 Royce places his left forearm in front of Gui's face and drives it down, forcing Gui's head to turn toward Royce's right hand.

7 Royce grabs the lapel with his left hand and drives the elbow down to the mat for the choke. Notice that Royce's lapel is tightly wrapped around Gui's neck, so when he drives the elbow to the mat, applying his weight behind it, he tightens the noose for a powerful choke.

86. Lapel choke 2: across-side variation

Another highly effective option for the lapel choke from the mount that Royce favors is to jump out of the mount to across-side. This variation is equally effective as the one shown in technique 85; it is simply a matter of preference which you use. We start the position with Royce already mounted and with the left lapel under Gui's neck, as in 85.3.

1 Royce is mounted on Gui and has wrapped his left lapel under Gui's head with his left arm.

2 Royce exchanges the grip on the lapel from his left hand to his right one. Notice that this time he does not lean to his left to feed the collar through.

3 While still gripping the lapel with his right hand, Royce braces off his left forearm and dismounts, stepping over and around with his right leg.

4 Royce reaches Gui's right side, his left hand planted on the ground as pivot and balance point, his right hand gripping the lapel. Royce drives the right elbow down to the mat for the choke. Notice how Royce's lapel is wrapped around Gui's neck.

5 Royce circles to his left. He will drive the right elbow to the ground if he needs to apply extra pressure on the choke.

87. Taking the back
(opponent tries to bridge)

As soon as you mount an opponent, his first reactions are to protect himself and try to escape, not necessarily in that order. The bridge, or upa, is perhaps the most common escape from the mount; it will be one of the first things your opponent tries as soon as you achieve the mount. Generally the upa is used as soon as you allow your opponent to control one of your arms. Since you are in a match and submission is one of the main objectives, it stands to reason that you will try to choke the opponent, giving him the opportunity to grab one of your arms. Being alert to the dynamics of the fight is one of the things that Royce emphasizes the most. Being able to predict and quickly react to what your opponent does is one of the keys to success in jiu-jitsu. In the case of the mount, in your mind you need to expect that your opponent will try to upa as soon as you try to choke. There are several counters to the upa, like grapevining your legs with your opponent's legs, but Royce's favorite is to take the back.

1 Royce has mounted Gui and is preparing a choke. Royce has his left hand on Gui's left shoulder (or he could have it grabbing the inside of the left collar), but Gui, being a smart fighter, has already initiated his upa escape. With his left hand, he grabs Royce's left wrist to release the pressure on his neck. With his right hand, he locks Royce's arm against his chest by pulling down on the biceps. At this point, Gui would begin to bridge to his own right. If Royce doesn't react quickly, he will be rolled over and end up on the bottom with Gui in his guard.

2 Royce opens the right knee slightly and shifts his weight to his own right. At the same time, he uses his right hand to push Gui's left elbow in and locks it in place by pressing down with his chest. Once Gui's left elbow is locked, he cannot pull it back out.

3 Royce continues to press his chest down on Gui's left arm, driving the elbow further to Royce's left. Notice that Royce has used his left hand to keep Gui's left forearm in control and prevent him from circling the arm around his head and releasing it back to the left. Notice also that at this point Gui's arm is locked against the mat; his left elbow is trapped by Royce's chest and his left hand is pressing against the mat. Royce could easily apply a wrist lock by pressing the left elbow up with his chest, forcing the forearm up against the top of the hand.

4 Instead, Royce prefers to take the back. He reaches with his right arm around Gui's head until he grabs the left wrist. The entire time, Royce uses his left hand to control Gui's left wrist and keep him from freeing it by circling up. Royce's chest is pressing against Gui's arm the entire time, locking it in place.

5 Royce uses his left hand to push down on Gui's left elbow. At the same time, he pulls Gui's left wrist around with his right hand. Royce opens his left leg slightly to create some space to turn Gui over. Royce needs to allow the space to make it easier to turn Gui over on his stomach.

6 Royce shifts his weight over to his right as he slides his right knee out and opens his left leg, giving Gui the necessary space to turn over. Royce is not worried about Gui escaping the position, as he has total control over Gui's upper body. Royce places his chest against the back of Gui's left shoulder. At this point, Royce can apply any of the side-mount attacks shown in that section.

7 Royce continues to turn Gui over by driving his chest forward against Gui's left shoulder, while at the same time pulling the left wrist with his right hand and pushing Gui's left elbow with his left hand. Notice how Royce has his legs in a wide base. The space he allows makes it easy to turn Gui over.

8 Royce completes the move, ending up in the back mount.

88. Double attack

So much of fighting involves throwing your opponent off his plan. Having multiple threats from the mount forces your opponent to make difficult decisions and yield something. In this case, Royce begins with a choke. When Gui defends it, he exposes his arm. Should Gui not defend the first attack, Royce would finish him with the choke.

1 Royce is mounted on Gui. He begins the double attack with an NHB choke, holding Gui's left shoulder with his left hand and driving his elbow down to the ground, forcing his forearm against Gui's neck. If this were a sport jiu-jitsu match, Royce would opt for having his right hand grab the inside of Gui's left collar. Gui counters the choke with both hands, grabbing each side of Royce's left forearm and pulling the elbow back to relieve the pressure on his neck.

2 Reacting to Gui's defense and the fact that Gui's left elbow is now up as he reached to grab Royce's left arm, Royce slides his left knee up toward Gui's head as far as he can, using his right hand on the ground for base. Notice that Royce opened his left leg slightly and slid his hips forward, trapping Gui's left arm with it as he moved toward Gui's left side. At this point, Royce has Gui in the double attack: Should Gui decide to defend the left arm and release the grip on Royce's left forearm, Royce would simply use his right hand on Gui's right shoulder (or collar) to choke him with a cross-choke.

3 Royce plants his right hand in front of Gui's head as he continues to slide his left knee up toward Gui's head and drive his hips forward, further trapping the left arm. Royce turns Gui over to the right by pulling the left shoulder with his left hand, making it easier for him to circle his leg over Gui's head. Notice that Royce's right hand planted on the ground not only keeps Gui from circling to his right to defend the armlock, but also serves as a pivot point for Royce to brace his body and circle his right leg over Gui for the armlock. At this point Royce is ready for the armlock. Notice his left knee is up and slightly bent on top of Gui's right side, ready for the submission.

4 Pivoting off his right hand, Royce circles his right leg over Gui's head.

5 Once he has his right leg locked over Gui's head, Royce sits on the mat to the left side of Gui, bringing his knees together. Royce uses his right hand on Gui's left shoulder to keep his hips tight, taking away any space for Gui to yank his arm out.

6 Royce leans back, taking Gui's left arm with him, and applies pressure on the elbow joint by driving his hips up as he pulls the wrist down. Notice that Royce's legs keep Gui's head and torso pinned to the ground, preventing him from rolling over to his left and stacking Royce to defend the armlock.

ARMLOCK TRICKS

Many times when you reach the armlock position, you have to deal with the opponent's last gasp of defense—grabbing his hands together in various configurations to avoid having his arm extended for the armlock. In this era of supersized competitors, facing a giant with biceps the size of thighs is not uncommon, so you needs to have a few tricks to pry the arms open. The next five positions demonstrate Royce's favorite ways for dealing with the most common situations.

89. Armlock 1:
Opponent clasps hands together

In this case, the opponent grabs his hands together, interlocking the fingers or simply locking the palms together. This is a fairly common occurrence and Royce has a clever way to deal with it.

1 Royce has reached the perfect armlock position. He has trapped Gui's left arm between his legs. His right arm is braced back to prevent Gui from rolling to his left and stacking him. His hips are close to Gui's shoulder, taking away any space for Gui to yank his elbow down and out. His left arm is wrapped around Gui's left arm, holding his own lapel to apply pressure to split the hands as he leans back with his torso. Gui is a very strong fighter, however, and has stubbornly resisted the pressure to break the hands apart.

2 Royce places his left foot on Gui's right arm and uses his right hand on Gui's left wrist.

3 At the same time, Royce leans back with his torso, forcing his left forearm up and back against Gui's left forearm. He pushes forward with his left leg against Gui's arm and pulls up on the wrist with his right hand. Since the power of the leg is stronger than most arms, and the torso leaning back causes pressure up and back, Gui has no option but to break the grip.

90. Armlock 2:
Opponent grabs one wrist

In this case, Gui grabs his left wrist with his right hand. The grip is very strong, sometimes even stronger than that demonstrated in technique 89. Royce can use the same technique he did there, but since the grip is stronger it may be harder to break. Royce opts for a clever solution instead.

1 Royce is ready to armlock Gui, but Gui holds his left wrist with his right hand to defend the attack. Royce has Gui's left arm wrapped by his right arm holding his own lapel.

2 Seeing that Gui has his left wrist unprotected, Royce reaches with his left hand and cups it over Gui's left hand without letting go of his right arm wrapped around Gui's arm.

3 Royce pulls Gui's left hand toward his own chest for a wrist lock. If Gui doesn't let go of the grip, he will submit to the wrist lock.

3 *Detail* Notice Royce's grip at the edge of Gui's hand for extra leverage. The further out he grabs, the more leverage he has on the wrist lock.

4 Gui has no option but to break the grip and Royce extends the arm.

91. Armlock 3:
Opponent grabs both wrists

This time, Gui defends breaking the grip by holding his wrists with the opposite hands, locking the arms together. Since the wrists are protected, the wrist-lock option is not available. Even if it was, gripping the wrists makes this counter stronger than simply clasping the hands and it cannot be broken as in technique 89. Although it may seem fairly easy to break any of these grips shown in this section, the reality of it when facing a strong and determined opponent is very different. If he feels he can muscle his defense, then he can start to bridge and roll to try to escape from the position. In this instance, Gui has his arms very close to his chest.

1 Royce has Gui's left arm wrapped with his own left arm. His right arm is back for brace and he is ready to extend the arm for an armlock. This time, however, Gui has countered by grabbing his wrists with the opposite hand, forming a strong lock. Royce begins by moving his left hand from his lapel to the top of his right thigh.

2 Royce loops his left leg over Gui's wrist ensemble. Notice that he uses his right hand to help pull the lower leg in place over the wrists.

3 Royce brings his right hand back to the mat for base and locks his right leg over the left foot, forming a figure-four around Gui's left arm over the wrists. When he crosses the triangle, Royce creates tremendous pressure on Gui's left elbow.

4 The pressure forces Gui to release the grip or suffer damage to his elbow or forearm.

92. Armlock 4: Opponent grabs both wrists (more space available)

In technique 91, Gui held his own wrists to prevent Royce from breaking the grip and finalizing the armlock. Gui had his arms very close to his chest, making the previous technique the best choice. Here, however, Gui has left some space between his arms and chest, allowing Royce to go for this triangle submission.

1 Royce is ready to apply the armlock and Gui's last resort is to lock his wrists with his hands, preventing Royce from straightening the arm for the armlock. Notice that in this case Gui's arms are slightly away from his chest, allowing Royce the space necessary for this technique.

2 Royce slips his left foot inside the gap formed by Gui's arms and his chest. Should Gui have held his arms close to the chest, Royce would have used technique 91. Notice that Royce slides his foot, with the toes pointed and the sole of the foot facing Gui's face. To do this without alerting Gui to what he is doing, he blocks Gui's vision by pushing down with his right leg against Gui's face.

3 Royce removes his right leg from Gui's face, allowing him to feel that he can turn toward Royce and pull his elbow out to defend the armlock.

4 Royce allows Gui to turn in, then pulls his head with the right hand as he opens his legs, trapping Gui's arm and head between the legs for the triangle.

5 Royce locks the figure-four triangle around Gui's left arm and head and braces back with his right arm. Royce can either allow Gui to come over the top or keep him in the triangle right there. Either way, he will finish Gui with the choke.

93. Armlock 5: opponent grabs both wrists (armlock submission)

In this variation on technique 92, Royce is in a similar situation, but rather than going for the triangle, he prefers to simply break the grip and go for the regular armlock. He may choose this option because he doesn't want to give Gui any chances of escaping, and he feels that opening the leg will allow Gui too much space.

1 Royce is ready to apply the armlock and Gui's last resort is to lock his wrists with his hands, preventing Royce from straightening the arm for the armlock.

2 Royce slides his right arm inside the space between Gui's arms and chest. He slides the right arm until his elbow is under Gui's wrist.

3 Royce drives his left elbow down inside Gui's left arm near his own chest and opens the palms of his hands up.

4 Royce interlocks his hands so that the palms of the hands are touching. Notice that Royce has set up a very strong brace and he will simply use it to corkscrew and break Gui's grip. Royce leans back . . .

5 And breaks Gui's grip, prying Gui's hands away from his wrists where there is the least amount of grip, instead of trying to pull the hands apart.

SIDE MOUNT

The side mount is another very good position in a street fight or a jiu-jitsu match. Many times when you mount your opponent, he will turn sideways in an attempt to escape, and you need to transition to the side mount or lose the position. In the side mount it is extremely important to have the knee closest to the opponent's head as high as possible so you can have good base. The opposite knee should be up, with the foot planted on the ground and tight against the opponent's waist to prevent any space for him to escape. Keep your weight centered, with the bulk of the weight resting on the heel of the foot and the same hand on the ground. Should you have your weight too far forward, your opponent can easily pull you and roll you over. Notice how Royce's weight is distributed toward Gui's back, sitting on his right heel, and how he has his left foot and right hand providing a brace, preventing Gui from pulling him over and rolling forward to end up on top. Another important thing you should do when you reach the side mount is immediately attack the opponent's neck to keep him busy defending instead of trying to escape. Should your opponent concentrate on the escape, you will be ready for the submission.

94. Side-mount choke 1

Many times when reaching the side mount, your first option available will be the choke. As the opponent turns to one side, he will expose the opposite collar for an attack. Be ready for this and take advantage of the opening right away.

1 Royce has reached the side mount on Gui. As Gui turns to his own right, Royce grabs the left lapel with his left hand and pushes it down.

2 Royce loops his right arm around Gui's head and feeds the left lapel to the right hand. Royce grabs the collar as high and tight against Gui's neck as possible. He does so by sliding his right thumb in the collar and sliding the hand up as far as he can, while straightening out the collar with his left hand, making it like a handrail.

3 Royce slides his left arm under Gui's left arm as he drives his left hand behind Gui's head. Notice that Royce's hand is opened like a knife as he slides the blade of the hand behind Gui's head.

4 Royce applies the choking pressure by pulling the collar tight with his right hand as he continues to slide his left hand behind Gui's head, forcing it forward against the lapel. The choking pressure is intensified as Royce continues sliding the left hand down and forward on the back of Gui's head.

95. Side-mount choke 2: defender slides hips out

When you get the side mount, your opponent may quickly counter, grabbing the leg with both hands and sliding his hips to escape. In that case, the previous choke may not work, as your opponent can simply turn to his right and take away the choking pressure of the collar against his neck. To counter that, Royce changes to a variation of the grip.

1 Royce has a side mount on Gui and is attempting a collar choke. Gui quickly counters by grabbing Royce's left gi pants with his right hand and pushing the leg away, creating enough space to escape his hips and turn to his right, which releases the collar pressure on his neck.

2 Sensing he is losing the pressure, Royce quickly changes his grip. Instead of having his left arm wrapped around Gui's neck, Royce's left hand reaches down and grabs Gui's right collar.

3 With his hands controlling both collars, Royce knows that Gui cannot escape the choke. He applies the choking pressure by pulling down on the right lapel with his left hand, straightening the lapel as he cinches the choke, and pulling up on the left lapel with his right hand. Notice that it is the right hand pulling Gui's left lapel that chokes him, but Royce's left hand straightening the opposite lapel takes away the slack for the powerful choke.

3 *Detail* Notice Royce's hands gripping Gui's lapel. His right hand is as high and tight on the left lapel as possible, and his left one grabs the right lapel slightly lower. The right-hand grip is the choking grip and needs to be tight around the neck. The left hand can grab lower on the gi, because it is only used to pull the collar down and tighten the noose around the neck.

96. Side-mount choke 3:
transition to back mount

As stated before, one of the first things that the attacker should do *after* he controls the side mount is attack the collar for a choke. Many times an experienced opponent will anticipate that and use his hand to protect the collar grab. In that case, depending on the hand position, one can take the back or go for an armlock. Here, since Gui maintains his left arm close to his chest, Royce takes the back and goes for a *mata leão* ("lion killer") choke. If he had some distance between the arm and his chest, Royce would opt for the armlock.

1 Royce has reached the side mount on Gui. Gui is on his right side and is using his left hand close to his chest to block Royce's right hand from reaching around his head and grabbing the left lapel for the choke. At the same time, Gui is working on his escape. With his right hand, he grabs Royce's left gi pants and pushes the leg away, trying to create some space for a hip escape. Should Royce fail to act, Gui will escape the side mount, so Royce grabs Gui's left wrist with his left hand and feeds it to his right one.

2 Once he has grabbed Gui's wrist with his right hand, Royce uses his left hand to push down on Gui's left arm near the elbow, forcing him to turn over.

3 Royce continues to force Gui to turn to his back by pulling on the left wrist with his right hand and pushing Gui's left elbow with his left hand. Notice how Royce shifted his weight back toward his right heel to release the pressure and allow space for Gui to turn over. Should Royce remain very tight against Gui's body, he would make it harder to force Gui to turn over. Royce is not concerned about losing the position; he has total control over Gui's upper body by controlling the left arm and driving his chest against Gui's back when necessary.

4 Royce continues forcing Gui to turn over, without releasing the right hand grip on Gui's left wrist. Royce uses his left hand on the mat for base and puts both knees down on the mat. Royce uses his chest to push down on Gui's back, trapping the left arm under his own body.

5 Having trapped Gui's left arm, Royce releases his right hand from Gui's left wrist and wraps it around the neck, leaving his hand open.

6 Royce locks his right hand on the left biceps and places his left hand behind Gui's head for the choke. Royce applies the choking pressure for the *mata leão* by bringing his elbows together and driving his chest forward and head down, while pushing forward with his left hand on the back of Gui's neck. One of the ways to visualize the pressuring movement is to imagine that you are hugging a longtime friend, except in this case you squeeze his neck. The actual pressure from this choke is tremendous; should Gui not submit in seconds, he will be out!

97. Side mount to armlock

In technique 96, Royce opted to go for the back mount because Gui was protecting the collar with his left hand and his left arm was tight against his chest. Many times, however, either the opponent will have his arm slightly opened or, in the scramble of positions, his arm will open, allowing for the armlock.

1 Royce has the side mount on Gui and is turning Gui around. Royce uses his chest to push Gui's left shoulder around as he grabs Gui's left wrist with his right hand. With his left hand, Royce pushes down on Gui's left elbow to turn him over.

2 Royce notices that Gui's arm is separated from his chest, so he reaches with his left arm inside the space between Gui's left arm and chest and grabs his own right wrist with the left hand.

3 Royce braces and pivots off his hands, pressing down and locking Gui's left wrist to the mat. He slides his right knee up toward Gui's head and brings his left foot in next to the hip, as he has his lower leg pointing straight up.

4 Still pivoting off his hands, Royce swings his right leg around over Gui's head. Notice how Royce's weight is on the frame formed by his hands, his head slightly over the frame. This makes it easy for Royce to swing the right leg around, as his weight is on the hands and not on the legs.

5 Once Royce's right leg touches the front of Gui's face, Royce falls back for the armlock. Notice Royce's legs on each side of Gui's left arm. The right leg presses down on the head so Gui can't turn into Royce and stack him, and the left leg pushes down on the chest to keep Gui from turning to his left in another attempt to escape the armlock.

6 Royce leans back all the way to the mat. His hips thrust up against Gui's left elbow for the submission.

98. Side mount to taking the back

Having multiple options from any position will make your game much more effective, be it a street fight or sport jiu-jitsu. Being able to quickly switch between options is even better. Feigning one possible attack and quickly switching to another will not only give you extra milliseconds in both decision-making and execution, but will also allow you to constantly surprise your opponent. If you have only one or two attacks, your opponent will only need to defend those; however, if you have three or four different attacks, it makes him uncertain what to defend. In this technique, Royce presents another alternative from the side mount: taking the back. Royce uses a very similar setup to the armlock, but surprises the opponent by pulling him over and taking the back.

1 Royce has the side mount on Gui, his left foot locked near Gui's hips and his right arm wrapped around Gui's head, with the hand locked around Gui's left wrist. Royce has slipped his left arm between Gui's left arm and chest and grips the wrist with his left hand as well. From this point Royce has many options, many of which have been shown in previous techniques. He can go to the armlock, can roll Gui for the back mount, or can take the back, as he does here.

2 Pivoting off the frame made by his arms and hands, Royce slides his right knee toward Gui's head, placing his right foot as close to Gui's back as possible to set up the next move. Royce leans forward as if he is going to apply the armlock.

2 *Incorrect stance* Royce's right foot is planted away from Gui's back, actually preventing Royce from sitting back.

2 *Correct stance* Notice how Royce brings his leg and foot next to Gui's back. This will allow the right foot to come out and hook as Royce pulls Gui over the top for back control.

3 In a surprise move, Royce sits back toward the mat, pulling Gui with him. Notice that Royce's arms are also locked around Gui's torso, so as he leans back he brings Gui with him.

4 Royce continues to sit back toward the mat, pulling Gui on top of him. Notice that Royce's left foot is already hooked over the hip for one hook, while his right foot is coming around to the front as he pulls Gui over the right leg and on top of him.

5 Royce rotates his body toward his right and loops the right leg over, locking his right foot on Gui's right hip and taking the back.

BACK ATTACKS

Having someone's back (with hooks or a back mount) is arguably the best position one can have. In jiu-jitsu competition you get the maximum points (4) for the position, and in a street fight or an NHB match it is tantamount to a win. You are behind the opponent with many options for strikes and submissions. Your opponent is not capable of seeing what you are doing, which is a great advantage. When having someone's back, the initial goal is to secure and maintain this valuable position.

99. Back submissions

Here Royce presents a sampling of the most common attacks from the back.

1 *Rear naked choke:* Royce wraps his right arm around Gui's neck, locking his right hand on his left biceps. He then locks his left hand behind Gui's head. Royce applies the choking pressure by collapsing everything around Gui's neck. He brings his elbows together and pulls them in the direction of his chest. He pushes forward with his chest and head, forcing Gui's head forward.

2 *Collar choke:* Royce reaches around Gui's neck with his right hand and grabs the left lapel. Royce wraps his left arm around Gui's left arm and drives his left hand behind the head. To apply the choking pressure, Royce pulls back the lapel with his right hand and slides his left arm behind Gui's head, as if he wants to straighten the arm. The motion is like drawing a bow, with the left hand holding the bow and the right hand pulling the cord. Notice that it is the right arm that chokes, so the right hand grip should be as deep as possible into the collar.

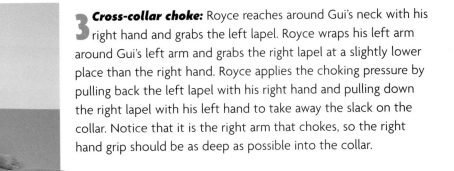

3 ***Cross-collar choke:*** Royce reaches around Gui's neck with his right hand and grabs the left lapel. Royce wraps his left arm around Gui's left arm and grabs the right lapel at a slightly lower place than the right hand. Royce applies the choking pressure by pulling back the left lapel with his right hand and pulling down the right lapel with his left hand to take away the slack on the collar. Notice that it is the right arm that chokes, so the right hand grip should be as deep as possible into the collar.

3 ***Correct position*** Notice Royce's right hand. The thumb is inside the collar and the blade of the forearm is against Gui's neck. The narrow blade makes for greater pressure. Royce's wrist is stiff and not bent, which would reduce the pressure against the neck.

3 ***Incorrect position*** Notice how Royce has his wrist turned forward, placing the wide part of his forearm against Gui's neck. The wider blade dissipates the choking pressure.

Important detail for all collar chokes

Correct grip
Notice how Royce grips the lapel. He wraps his fingers and bends the collar around, making a better grip and creating a blade with the collar against the neck. Note that Royce actually drives the inside part of the collar against the neck, not the outside of the collar.

Incorrect grip
Royce doesn't turn the collar and actually pulls the wide part of the collar against Gui's neck.

100. Rear naked choke 1:
opponent blocks the choking arm

Many times when you attempt a rear naked choke, your opponent will block the choke by grabbing the choking arm with both hands and pulling it down, preventing you from locking your arm around his neck. Royce shows a clever solution to the problem.

1 Royce has Gui's back with hooks in place and is attempting the rear naked choke. Gui counters by grabbing Royce's right forearm with both hands to keep him from locking the choke.

2 Royce moves his left arm over Gui's left arm. His left palm is open.

3 Royce places the left hand on top of Gui's right hand and pushes it down for a wrist lock. Notice that Gui's right elbow is blocked from moving by Royce's right leg and hips. Gui has to release the grip or submit to the wrist lock.

4 Royce slides his right arm deep around Gui's neck and is ready to complete the rear naked choke demonstrated in technique 99.

101. Rear naked choke 2: opponent blocks the choking arm (arm-change variation)

Here is an alternative to technique 100 for situations when the opponent prevents the choking arm from locking deep around his neck. Royce makes use of his gi to open space for a change of arms.

1 Royce has Gui's back, hooks in place, and tries for a rear naked choke, but Gui blocks Royce's right arm from coming around his neck, pulling down on Royce's forearm with both hands. Royce locks his right hand behind Gui's left shoulder to keep him from pulling the forearm too far down.

2 He then grabs his own left gi lapel with his left hand and feeds it to the right hand. Notice that since Royce's right hand was already on Gui's shoulder, it is only a short distance to the lapel.

3 Royce leans back, driving the right arm under Gui's chin to force Gui's head up, creating the necessary space for Royce's left hand to slide between Gui's left arm and chest. Notice that Royce has his left hand in a blade, making it easier to slip into a narrow gap.

4 Royce drives his left arm completely around Gui's neck. Once he has his left hand clear on the right side of Gui's body, he starts to release his right arm, allowing Gui to pull it down.

5 As Gui pulls Royce's right arm down, it creates the space for Royce to quickly slide his left palm over the right biceps, locking it for the choke.

102. Rear naked choke 3: opponent blocks the choking arm (armlock variation)

A seldom-used option to deal with the rear-naked-choke counter is to go for the armlock. Although it is slightly riskier, because you release a lot of your back control, this move works surprisingly well because of the element of surprise. Remember, when applying surprise moves, make sure you have the execution of the move down by having practiced it many times prior to actually trying it against an unwilling opponent.

1 Royce has Gui's back with hooks on and is attempting a rear naked choke with his left arm around Gui's neck. Gui counters the attack, locking both hands on Royce's forearm and pulling it down.

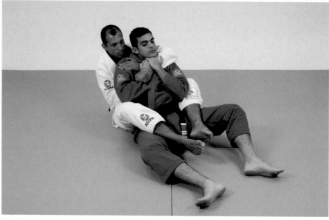

2 Royce brings his right knee up, driving Gui's right elbow slightly away from his body. This opens a gap between the arm and the body, allowing Royce to slide his right arm inside and grab Gui's right wrist.

3 In control of Gui's right wrist, Royce spins his body to his right, releasing the left foot hook from Gui's hip and spinning until his right foot hooks the outside of Gui's left thigh. Notice that Royce continues with his left arm, trying to complete the choke and forcing Gui to continue grabbing that arm.

4 Royce uses his right leg as a pivot point as he releases the left arm off Gui's neck and brings it around the back of the head. Notice that Royce uses the right leg pushing off the right foot hook to help bring his body around.

5 Royce makes a frame with his left forearm against Gui's face, preventing him from turning into him and reaching guard, but also maintaining the proper distance so he can execute the armlock. Royce continues turning to his right as he swings the left leg around Gui's head.

6 Royce brings his left leg in front of Gui's face and presses it down, forcing Gui back. He then releases the left forearm from the face and brings it back to control Gui's right wrist.

7 Royce's left leg pressing down on Gui's head forces Gui back to the mat. Royce is in perfect position for the armlock.

8 Royce leans back and extends Gui's arm back with him as he drives his hips up, hyperextending the elbow for the submission.

103. Rear naked choke 4:
opponent blocks the second arm (NHB option)

In the preceding chokes, even if your opponent fails to block the choking arm from wrapping around his neck, he still has a chance to prevent your second arm from locking the hold. Royce demonstrates the NHB option to deal with the situation: heel strikes to the opponent's stomach.

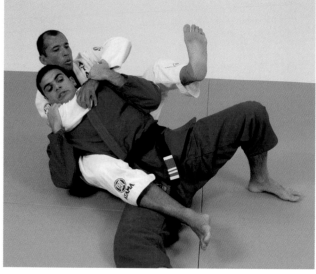

1 Royce has Gui's back with hooks in place. He got ahead of Gui and was able to reach around the neck with his right arm, but as he brings in his left arm to lock the choke, Gui counters, blocking it with his left hand grabbing Royce's left wrist.

2 Since Royce is choking with the right arm, Gui's escape route would be to slide to his left. Knowing that, Royce turns to his right and has Gui leaning to that side, making it more difficult for him to escape to the left. Because of that, Royce opens his left leg, releasing the hook, and lifts it up.

3 Royce brings his heel down, striking Gui's stomach.

4 Royce repeats the movement as many times as necessary for Gui to release the arm.

5 As soon as Gui releases his grip to block the heel strikes, Royce locks his rear naked choke by grabbing his own left biceps with the right hand, placing his left hand behind Gui's head, and applying the choke.

104. Rear naked choke 5:
opponent blocks the second arm
(jiu-jitsu option)

If rules prevent you from applying the heel strikes used in technique 103, use this option to end the fight.

1 Royce has Gui's back with hooks in place. He got ahead of Gui and was able to reach around the neck with his right arm, but as he brings in his left arm to lock the choke, Gui counters, blocking it with both hands grabbing Royce's left wrist.

2 Royce leans forward with his head and upper body and reaches around Gui's neck with his right arm until he can lock the palm of his right hand behind his own neck or head.

2 *Detail* Notice how Royce grabs the back of his neck with the palm of his hand. Royce turns his head to his left to make it easier for him to reach the back of the neck.

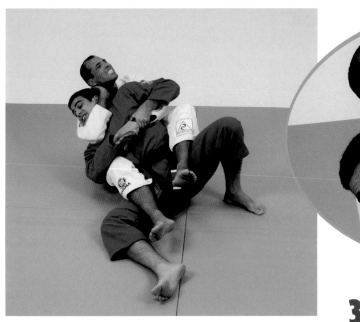

3 Royce leans back with his head and torso, brings his right arm with them, and cinches the choke on Gui.

3 *Detail* Notice how Royce leans back and to his right with the head, tightening the choke around Gui's neck.

Gracie Jiu-Jitsu Positional Ladder

Throw

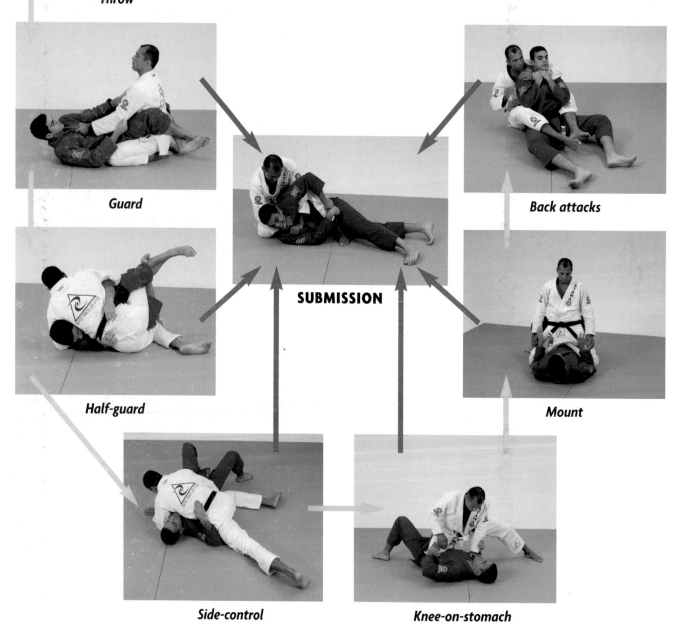

Guard

Half-guard

SUBMISSION

Back attacks

Mount

Side-control

Knee-on-stomach